1+1=7

How Smart Leaders Make
7 Investments
to Maximize Value

Baldwin H. Tom

INDIE BOOKS
INTERNATIONAL

1+1=7™ is a trademark of Baldwin H. Tom

ISBN: 10: 1-947480-11-1
ISBN: 13: 978-1-947480-11-7
Library of Congress Control Number: 2018930939

Designed by Joni McPherson, mcphersongraphics.com

INDIE BOOKS INTERNATIONAL, LLC
2424 VISTA WAY, SUITE 316
OCEANSIDE, CA 92054
www.indiebooksintl.com

DEDICATION

This book is dedicated to God, who sustains me; to my wife, who cares for me; and to my family and friends, who support me.

TABLE OF CONTENTS

PREFACE

One of my early assignments as an independent management consultant was to determine the value or cost of failed training for insurance agents and to present the results. If the company spent time and money to train a new agent, and the trainee left at the end of the year, what was the cost (loss) to the agency?

That was an easy assignment. I simply added the cost of hours for training, salaries, materials, and customer considerations that I had gathered from the agency and totaled those up to reach a number. At that time, twenty years ago, the minimal loss was $100,000 per failed trainee. It was a shocker for the agency; they had not made the computations before.

That experience led to another assignment: to compute the value or cost of *morale* (or lack thereof). This was a more challenging task, but to help compute this, I came up with another algorithm. From that point forward, I felt able to quantify all soft-side, intangible aspects of a business. Along the way, I became aware that businesses do not account for such intangibles. Standard financial statements do not include people as assets, even though, without people, there would *be* no business.

It was not a great leap for me to become interested in helping business leaders analyze and optimize intangible investments within enterprises, as people are investments. Thus began my journey to consider intangible investment types and their roles in creating high Return-on-Investment (ROI).

Thank you for joining me on this journey.

Baldwin H. Tom
April 2018

CHAPTER 1

THINK INVESTMENTS, NOT BUSINESS VALUATION

Leaders need to know hidden wealth resides in organizations: their people, their creativity, and their leveraged interactions. This book is all about helping leaders find that hidden wealth and leverage investments in their businesses to gain enhanced value and ROI.

The challenge is that many leaders do not fully appreciate the totality of where the value resides in their organizations.

If there were a way to clearly see the different

investment types in a business enterprise, would you be interested?

If you answered "yes," there is good news. The goal of this book is not to provide a new way to value a business, but to show where value is typically not realized within a business. Why is this important? Because if leaders understand the seven best areas in which to invest in their companies, then they can greatly increase the value of those businesses.

Before such a discussion begins, however, it is important to address how investments (both tangible [task-side] and intangible [people-side]) fit into valuation. Standard accounting practices are available to compute and characterize tangible assets in a business. For example, the balance sheet tabulates Assets and Liabilities. Intangible investments, on the other hand, have no standard measures or tracking mechanisms.

Where Value Hides in Plain Sight

Think of this book like a treasure map; it will help you find hidden riches or assets. The discussion begins with how accountants traditionally account for assets.

While they know how to account for tangible assets, accounting for the value of intangible assets in a business has been a historical challenge. This includes the value people bring to the company (e.g., education, training, expertise, experiences, and certifications) along with what they do to add value to an enterprise, such as building corporate knowledge (processes, procedures, norms, and inventions). In addition, intangible assets include intellectual property (e.g., patents, trademarks, and copyrights), relationships (both interpersonal and customer), and goodwill. Within this context, the concept of intellectual capital has been defined as all those intangibles that consist of people and/or are derived from a business's people.

Now consider questions that arise regarding intangible assets as they relate to the other two standard accounting statements that describe a business's financials—cash flow and income statements. How will intangible assets be entered into the cash flow statement, which tracks the inflow and outflow of a company's money? What portion of funds is obtained from the intangible component of the business, and what amount is used? For the income statement, how are revenues and expenses from intangible investments logged? Accountants are undertaking ongoing efforts to answer these questions with studies that seek to capture the intangible assets into a company's financials. Yet it will take time before the accounting community accepts and formalizes consensus on algorithms and methods. Until then, valuation of intangibles will be provided in multiple ways, or not at all.

The current solution for determining the value of intangible assets is simple. The challenge is determining agreement on how to (1) characterize the intangibles, (2) agree on numerical values for the intangibles, and (3) agree on how to incorporate intangible assets into the financials.

The first step is to consider the connection of intangible assets with intellectual capital, which is covered in the next chapter.

There exists untapped value in every organization hidden in people and what they do.

CHAPTER 2

INTANGIBLE ASSETS AND INTELLECTUAL CAPITAL, DEFINED

B efore you can uncover hidden wealth, it helps to know what you are looking for.

Ever since I first heard the phrase, "Our people are our greatest assets," I have wondered why there is no place on financial statements to account for their value. To understand this, let's begin the discussion by defining our terms.

Intangible Assets, Defined

Yes, people are assets. Until recently, however, the accounting world did not consider the value of intangible assets in business financials. This clearly suggests that whenever financial data are presented, they are necessarily incomplete, because they do not include the value of intangible assets: people and what they provide. The term "intellectual capital" (IC) is now being used to encompass the intangible, people-derived assets of a business.

Early definitions of IC included:

- IC is the value of a business that exceeds the value of its tangible (physical and financial) assets (in other words, total business value minus physical + financial value = IC).[1]

- IC is all the identifiable nonmonetary assets without physical substance.[2]

- IC is everything left behind when employees go home.[3]

Intellectual Capital, Defined

The first use of the term "Intellectual Capital" is attributed to the late Harvard professor and economist,

---

[1] Magrassi, Paolo. "A Taxonomy of Intellectual Capital." 2002. Gartner.com.

[2] The International Financial Reporting Standards (IFRS) committee developed the International Accounting System 38 with the purpose of prescribing the accounting treatment for intangible assets. IAS 38.8 defines an intangible asset as an identifiable non-monetary asset without physical substance. https://www.iasplus.com/en/standards/ias/ias38

[3] Edvinsson, Leif and Michael S. Malone. *Intellectual Capital: Realizing Your Company's True Value by Finding its Hidden Brainpower.* Harper Business Press, New York, NY, 1997.

John Kenneth Galbraith, in 1967.[4] By the 1980s, academic discussion used the terms "knowledge capital" and "intangible assets" to cover the same topics. In the 1990s, Knowledge Management (KM) was coined to focus the importance of these intangible assets in a business. How does one transform innovations by people (human resources) into intellectual assets? The concept of KM during this time is found in publications and discussions from Holland, Sweden, Japan, and the United States. I like the definition published by Karl-Erik Sveiby, often described as one of the founding fathers of knowledge management, in the April 9, 1998, newsletter, *Intellectual Capital and Knowledge Management*: "the art of creating value from intangible assets."

Beyond defining what constitutes IC, managers and accountants have recently started working on ways to measure intangible assets. How does one assign numerical values to IC? While a search on the Internet reveals many studies and reports on IC, there is currently no definitive approach and certainly no accepted means to tabulate intangible assets on financial spreadsheets. Yet, there is no question that intangible assets add value to an enterprise.

---

[4] Galbraith, John Kenneth. *The New Industrial State*. Houghton Mifflin, Boston, 1967.

The Business Dictionary website defines Intellectual Capital as:

> Collective knowledge (whether or not documented) of the individuals in an organization or society. This knowledge can be used to produce wealth, multiply output of physical assets, gain competitive advantage, and/or to enhance value of other types of capital. IC is now beginning to be classified as a true capital cost because (1) investment in (and replacement of) people is tantamount to investment in machines and plants, and (2) expenses incurred in education and training (to maintain the shelf life of intellectual assets) are equivalent to depreciation costs of physical assets. Intellectual capital includes customer capital, human capital, intellectual property, and structural capital.[5]

Talent Valuation, by Thomas McGuire and Linda Brenner, further provides a clear understanding why talent, not just employee management, is the new value generator in this information age.[6] With talent, IC is created, and IC is what generates value for an enterprise. Competitive advantage is centered on creating, sustaining, and growing IC. McGuire and Brenner developed an algorithm for calculating the IC

---

[5] "What Is Intellectual Capital? Definition and Meaning." *BusinessDictionary.com*, www.businessdictionary.com/definition/intellectual-capital.html. Accessed September 16, 2017.

[6] McGuire, Thomas, and Linda Brenner. *Talent Valuation: Accelerate Market Capitalization through Your Most Important Asset*. Pearson Education Ltd., 2015.

value of publicly traded and nonprofit companies—their IC index.

My Story

The genesis of this book derives from three aspects of my life experiences. First, thirty years as an independent management consultant resulted in years of pent-up ideas in my head, along with the ability to see the forest from the trees and to integrate disparate information into a coherent framework.

Second, some people just have a gift for numbers and some don't. My lack of passion in numerical computations leads me to seek those who have a passion for numbers. In my business finance classes, I recognized I did not enjoy number crunching, but loved what numbers can tell us. I found analyzing financial ratios very interesting, just not the computations.

Finally, my fascination with intangible, soft-side metrics is an intrinsic part of who I am. In personality profiles, even though I am more task-oriented, I also have a strong need to see people as important—maybe it's my task-side need to quantify the intangible. Ever since I was first asked to help determine what *morale* was worth to a business, I was hooked on coming up with metrics that could be used to provide valuation for people and the intangibles they represent. I wanted to know what *fear,* or *satisfaction,* or *teamwork* was worth—or cost.

Collectively, these aspects challenged me to integrate the *people* and *task* sides of an enterprise, which then morphed into considering these as investments and how they might provide significant returns on investment.

Unfortunately, many attempts to achieve significant ROI fall short. Let's consider why in the next chapter.

Intellectual capital represents the collective wealth in an organization.

CHAPTER 3

WHY MOST INVESTMENTS FAIL TO REACH FULL POTENTIAL

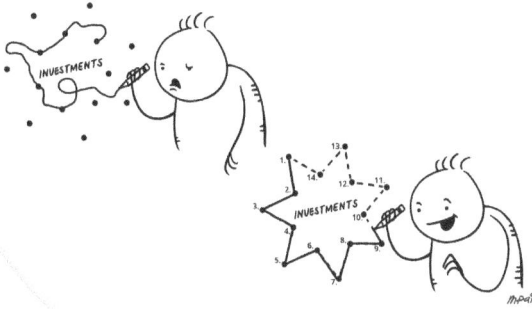

Investments—solutions to business needs—need to be clearly understood to be optimized. In every human endeavor, as in solving a problem, there are two components—the thing to be done and the people who do the thing. Put simply, there is a *task side* and a *people side* to the endeavor.[7] When we speak of investments, it is reasonable to consider whether they are on the task or people side. Are we investing on the task side with hard assets like tools and equipment,

---

[7] Tom, Baldwin H. and Ian C. Jacobsen. "Peter Principle Meets Doss Principle: Secrets for Engaging Consultants to Management." National Contract Management Association's *Journal of Contract Management*, Feb. 2006, 42-47.

or on the people side with training and counseling? This two-component idea can be used to display the different investments needed to get work done. When faced with multidimensional sets of ideas, such as the different investments, I like tables and graphs to help visualize and to present the information simply. I have used this approach in Table 1 to frame and explore this two-component thinking.

TABLE 1   Task/People Framing

Task Side	People Side
Tangibles	Intangibles
Hard assets	Soft assets
Work to be done	Those who do the work
Things	Interactions, teamwork
Structure, fixtures	Culture, norms

This framing simplifies problem-solving into two components. If there is a problem, one asks, "Which side of the frame is the problem?" For example, if a job is not being done well, is it due to a problem on the task or people side? If it is on the task side, then a lack of equipment or poor processes may be the problem. If it is on the people side, it may be a lack of training or education.

Let's take this another step by introducing another column that we call *linkage.*

Linkages facilitate, support, fund, or provide the currency of exchange between people and tasks. Linkages facilitate smooth processing—something like adding WD-40 lubricant to the process. Without appropriate linkage(s), an effort will be more difficult and the benefit (value) of the effort minimized.

TABLE 2   Task/People Framing with Linkage

Task	Linkage	People
Tangibles	Recipient of work (purpose)	Intangibles
Work to be done	Funds to facilitate work and interactions (means)	Those who do the work
Things	Environment through which work and interactions move (barriers)	Interactions
Structure, fixtures		Culture, norms

Meet the Magnificent Seven

Most organizations do not segment the idea of work into the categories of tasks, people, and linkages. While we all move through these stages in our endeavors, there is no deliberate focus on them. This lack of focus causes us to lose opportunities to create value in organizations.

When we sort work components into separate categories, we uncover seven different areas in the value-generating endeavor where we can invest time and effort and thus create ROI for an enterprise.

These seven areas are not new. Different consultants and authors have defined them and spoken about them—some in great detail. What I have done is to put them into a coherent framework. I have named these seven investments the Magnificent Seven (M-7) in honor of the original version of the 1960 movie, *The Magnificent Seven*. In the film, seven gunfighters join forces to help a small Mexican town rid itself of bandits. In the same way, I suggest that the M-7 framework will help a business optimize its value to beat the competition.

In Table 3, I have inserted M-7 investment categories into the Task/People matrix with short descriptors for each of the M-7. The M-7 includes four intangible, people-side categories (Human, Relational, Customer, and Spiritual) and three primarily tangible, task-side (Financial, Organizational, and Physical) categories. I have always said that people are more important than tasks, so this sorting into four people-side and three task-side groupings validates it. Besides, *people are our greatest assets,* right?

TABLE 3	Task/People Matrix with M-7 Categories	
Task	**Linkage**	**People**
Organizational	**Financial**	**Human**
Work we do and how we do it (processes, procedures, intellectual property, brand)	Funds to facilitate work and interactions (investments, debt funds, cash)	Those who do the work (training, education)
	Customer	
	Recipient of work (feedback, partnering)	
Physical	**Spiritual**	**Relationship**
Structure, fixtures, things, tangibles (equipment, software, facilities)	Environment through which work and interactions move (satisfaction, goodwill, morale, norms, culture)	Culture, norms, Interactions, Intangibles (teams, partners)

To get the best return on our investment in people requires leadership, which is the subject of the next chapter.

There are seven capital investments that produce organizational value and wealth.

CHAPTER 4
THE CHALLENGE FOR LEADERSHIP

L et's suggest that $1+1=7$, not 2. In business, the better I can leverage talents and resources, the more profitable my business will become. In other words, if I get a return on investment (ROI) greater than one, that's a worthy goal. One important challenge for leadership is to optimize the productivity of personnel. This gets me to the consideration that $1+1=7$, not 2. How is that? Normally, one person working together with another person equals two persons. However, as each person brings unique talents and experiences to a project, their collaboration leverages each person's abilities. Hence, the addition of $1+1$ cannot result in a sum of two; it becomes a multiple, or product, of two.

Here is additional rationale for this *higher math*.

In business, I would not want to be standing still, making no money, because without making more than it costs to do business, I cannot meet customers' needs, nor can I expand to provide better products or service. Therefore, I suggest that a $1+1=2$ mindset is what I call *status quo* math, in which a business is doing just enough to maintain, and each person is simply doing his or her own thing. Ultimately, this approach will cause the business to fail, because there will be no funds to move beyond status quo. (By the way, someone asked if it is possible that $1+1$ can be less than 2. Yes, absolutely, but that's a different discussion.)

As a business executive, a mindset of, $1+1=4$ is certainly better, but I would consider this a recipe for *transitional* change. That is, thinking and leveraging efforts in these terms, the business will have funds to grow, but only incrementally. Ideally, I am looking for *transformational* growth to beat the competition and to be the leader in my business's field.

This brings me to $1+1=7$. With this mindset, we recognize the need to maximize all seven investments in an enterprise. Said differently, we are talking about a ROI and how each of the M-7 investments support maximal returns. Leveraging these seven investments is the challenge for leadership.

While people may quibble with the leveraged multiplier, I chose $1+1=7$, leveraging the 2 to the third power, or $2^3 = 8$. Thus, two persons teaming together each provide inputs that produce a multiplier of 3. Conveniently, I lowered the 2^3 from 8 to 7 to fit my narrative of 7 investments. This is not mathematics, but leveraging investments. The ROI of two persons could be 2, 3, 4, or whatever number depending on who they are and what they know and how they perform. Hence, the $1+1$ can be 7. This is like fuzzy logic; It is fuzzy math.

The multiplier found in untapped value is exponential, where 1+1=7.

CHAPTER 5

THE MAGNIFICENT SEVEN INVESTMENTS— THE PEOPLE SIDE

Many people have heard the phrases "human capital," "relationship capital," and "spiritual capital." Many, however, are not certain what these terms mean in a practical sense.

Human Capital

Human capital in an organizational context refers to the collective value of the organization's intellectual capital, including knowledge, skills, and competencies. The value of human capital includes motivation, potential, and initiative. The *results* of human capital are found throughout an organization in organizational capital (patents, processes, procedures, etc.), in physical capital (innovative products and services), in spiritual capital (morale, work satisfaction, norms, etc.), and in relationship capital (teamwork, customer relations). Importantly, human capital results need to be captured and documented in processes, procedures, methods, and inventions (committed to corporate memory), or the value generated for the enterprise is lost when those with key talents depart the business.

Human Capital Investments

Investing in human capital is an easy one. Just as with physical capital investment, without upgrades, technology becomes slow and/or obsolete. Look at how software evolves; if you don't upgrade to new versions, eventually you will not be able to continue to function and communicate with the rest of the world. It is the same with people; we need continuous upgrades. Training, coaching, education (degrees), mentoring, and internships are all obvious ways to increase the value of a business's human capital. One frequently missed investment in this realm is when new technology is purchased and rolled out by a business with insufficient training for its people. The result? The new technology is not utilized to its full potential, and optimal ROI not realized.

Relationship Capital

One of the most valuable assets (if not *the* most valuable) in an organization is relationships. Value is derived and created daily within organizations from leveraging people's interactions. It's about power and influence. The network of people and organizations that represent the enterprise's customers, partners, suppliers, employees, former employees, and others with high levels of organizational influence constitute the participants in its relationship capital. Building relationships increases spiritual capital, "goodwill," an intangible asset that gives a customer comfort and confidence and facilitates doing business with the business. Building relationship capital delivers a host of ROI benefits:[8]

- **Business is sustained** because of relationships with customers.

- **Threats are identified** early because of solid relationships.

- **Cost-of-sales is reduced** because the cost of winning business from a new customer is four to seven times greater than winning more business from an existing customer.

---

[8] "What is Relationship Capital?" *Related Vision*. Accessed September 2017. http://www.relatedvision.com/Relationship-Capital/relationship-capital.html

- **Better margins are facilitated** because business happens more quickly, at what Stephen M.R. Covey calls "the Speed of Trust" in his book of the same name. There is less haggling as buyers trust you are charging a fair price (which means you can also more easily charge a fair price, not a cheap one).

- **People are better matched** to other people, e.g., matching salespeople to buyers on the basis of those best able to relate effectively, which increases the chances of customers buying from you.

- **Positive word-of-mouth increases,** providing the best promotion and source of referrals.

- **Customer retention increases,** reducing likelihood of customers switching to competitors, as there is no motivation to do so.

- **Happier customers lead to happier employees**, improving staff retention and reducing hiring and training costs.

Relationship Capital Investments

Investing in relationship capital generally brings benefits and ROI beyond expectations, because until a relationship is built, one does not know what other influencers the partnering relationship brings to the table. For this reason alone, we can consider relationship capital a very important area of investment. The multiplier for ROI may appear small, but secondary impact and synergies of relationships can be huge.

Spiritual Capital

Spiritual capital in a business derives from the values created by an organization's leadership and its cultural norms. This is not about religion, yet provides the same kind of peace, joy, and personal satisfaction that religion can, exhibiting and supporting what is important (values) to enrich lives. Captured within the category of spiritual capital is doing what is right and what is in the public interest rather than an exclusive focus on making profits. In a business with a great deal of spiritual capital, there is ethical decision-making built into a value-based culture where the goal is less shareholder gain and more gain for customers and stakeholders beyond the business. The culture engendered by such values produces norms within the organization that energizes and enriches the human spirit, fostering social connectedness and personal fulfillment. It spurs people to go the extra mile, to do whatever is needed versus what is contained in a defined workday. Such a culture, built around camaraderie and group chemistries, can make resolution of conflicts less confrontational, as civility is hardwired in the relationship.

Spiritual Capital Investments

This investment is a bit more complex; it entails an overt, proactive outlay of resources in outcomes that people care about which bring them personal satisfaction and a feeling of accomplishment. Spiritual investment has much to do with cultural norms and business practices. It is about ethical leadership and how people are treated. It is about consistency in leadership that leads to stable corporate morale and expectations fulfilled, i.e., no surprises. From a practical perspective, spiritual capital investments include efforts to demonstrate values through voluntarism and charitable donations. Such investments include a conscious effort to build a *family* culture that honors and supports each other and are demonstrated by the organization's efforts that they care about people. Spiritual capital is also built by investing in the well-being of personnel with concern about their families, including providing great employee benefits, contributing to company personnel in their volunteer efforts to help others, and building infrastructure and processes, like a reward system, that encourages high performance.

Customer Capital

Customer capital is simply the relationship value a business builds with its customers. Such value goes beyond customer loyalty and is derived from customer feedback to the business, partnering with the customer to produce new products and services. Value also manifests in the form of referrals and great press about the business from customers, the customers' customers, and their associates.

Customer Capital Investments

Without customers, where would we be? Every executive recognizes the importance of paying attention to the customer. But just being nice (sending holiday cards or gifts) is only a beginning when it comes to enhancing ROI. Making efforts to partner with the customer is the ideal investment. This can be done by engaging the customer to gain feedback, contributing to what the customer cares about, offering ways to improve products and services to better serve the customer, and joining with the customer to collectively create a new product or service.

In the next chapter, we will consider the task side of M-7 investments.

Investments in the four people-side capitals build Intellectual Capital and business value, but are currently not represented in financial statements.

CHAPTER 6

THE MAGNIFICENT SEVEN INVESTMENTS– THE TASK SIDE

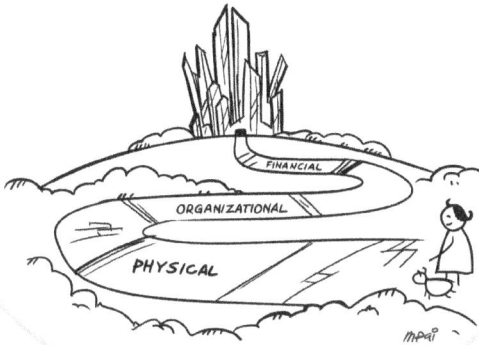

Organizational Capital

Organizational capital represents the value of an enterprise derived from mostly intangible assets such as processes, procedures, systems, patents, trade secrets, reputation, brand and intellectual property, plus "knowledge used to combine human skills and physical capital into systems for producing and delivering want-satisfying products."[9]

---

[9] Evans, Peter, et al. "Measuring Organizational Capital." *The Center for Global Enterprise,* 24 Feb. 2016, thecge.net/category/research/measuring-organization-al-capital/.

Organizational Capital Investments

One of the most important investments leaders can make is in organizational capital. This is where the memory of the enterprise resides. Building, investing in, and maintaining one's brand and reputation and protecting intellectual property (trade secrets, patents, processes, and procedures) are critical to sustaining the enterprise. This is where one protects the knowledge, skills, and expertise from being lost when talented people depart from the organization.

Physical Capital

Physical capital has historically been described under "capital investments" to characterize the *fixed* materials needed in producing products and services. This category includes physical things like machinery, buildings, equipment, computers, and other technology that, together with land and labor, turn raw materials into finished products and services. In reality, M-7 investments can be considered in aggregate as capital investments. Thus, physical investments, as well as the other six investments, are a subset of capital investments.

Physical Capital Investments

The benefits of investing in physical capital are self-evident. Without timely investment in equipment, technology, computers, etc., the enterprise would become noncompetitive and fail. It's important that we know that any investment in physical capital requires a commensurate investment on the people side—either in human, relationship, and/or customer capital, which will leverage this investment and optimize ROI.

Financial Capital

Financial capital is the monetary currency used to run the business, from acquiring materials to running operations. It is the currency of exchange between people and the things they need or do. It can be funds from interest returns, borrowed funds (debt equity), or funds derived from generating revenues via sales.

Financial Capital Investments

This is the traditional source for funding an enterprise. Thus, investments here support this funding effort. Funds on the financial side are documented in the financial statements of a business. There is little mystery here. Financial capital facilitates success of a business in its role purchasing materials/resources and investing in the people doing the work. Financial capital is one of two *currencies of exchange* between people who do the work and things they work on. The other *currency of exchange,* already mentioned, is on the intangible side—spiritual capital.

The task side, mostly tangible, investments are traditionally accounted for in financial statements.

CHAPTER 7

THE MAGNIFICENT SEVEN INVESTMENT–LINKAGES AND VALUE GENERATION

While I have outlined a seven-component investment scheme to delineate the areas of enterprise investment, this segmentation does not mean there are clean divisions among the investments.

Interactivity and Relationship of the M-7

When we are talking about intangibles, there are inevitable overlaps. Indeed, one investment may fit into more than one category of investment. Importantly, once the accounting profession determines a standardized approach to reporting intangible investments and value, there may yet be changes to where different intangibles fit on financial spreadsheets. In addition to overlaps, there are important interactions among the investments.

M-7 and Intellectual Capital

As noted in Chapter 2, IC is a category used to capture all investments that directly have to do with people and what they produce. While four of seven investments are directly people-oriented, Organizational Capital may also be added to this people group, as these are also people-derived products. Thus five out of seven (71 percent) of the investment categories are people-oriented. Importantly, the memory of an enterprise is collected and managed as Organizational Capital. When people speak about Knowledge Management, they are speaking about Human Capital, but more about the products contained within Organizational Capital, as all the processes and procedures, patents, trade secrets, and other intellectual properties are produced and collected there. Building value in a business enterprise requires investments in every one of the M-7 in different combinations. Investments are not only to make money and grow the business (products, services, and customers), but also to grow and sustain the inner workings of the entity (corporate memory, innovations, resiliency, and sustainability). This latter activity builds wealth for the entity.

M-7 as a Body

As I considered the interrelationships and linkages of different investments, it became apparent that these interactions cross-pollinate in every way. Each investment is one part of the whole, much like the coordinated workings of a body.

1. Human capital: Brain

2. Relationship capital: Heart

3. Spiritual capital: Soul (mind, emotion, will)

4. Customer capital: Purpose

5. Organizational capital: Memory

6. Financial capital: Blood

7. Physical capital: Hands and feet

This potential for interinvestment coordination reinforces the obvious: that each investment has an important role to play in the enterprise, depending on the purpose and point of view. Not all parts are emphasized at the same time in the same way. Depending on the need, different parts are activated, just as they are in the examples below.

Selective Investments Support the Enterprise

Item	Investments Support	Supported by M-7 Investments
1	Leadership and Management	HC (Human Capital)+SC (Spiritual C); HC+OC (Organizational C)
2	Communication and Culture	SC+RC (Relationship C)
3	Resiliency and Sustainability	RC+SC; HC+SC; CC (Customer C)+OC
4	Creativity and Innovation	HC+CC; RC+CC; HC+SC
5	Intellectual Property and Corporate Memory	HC+OC
6	New Products and Services	FC (Financial C); FC+HC; FC+RC; FC+SC; FC+CC; FC+PC (Physical C); FC+OC

Leadership and Management

What investments support leadership and management styles?

- *Human capital—Spiritual capital* investments are important because expectations developed within the organization's culture form expectations about governance. Thus, leadership issues focus around these two forms of capital.

- *Human capital—Organizational capital* investments play roles in the type of leadership and management as process, procedures, and operational norms guide governance.

- The behavior of people (human capital) and how they feel (spiritual capital) about the organization, along with how they go about dealing with issues and each other, reflect how they are managed and led.

Communication and Culture

What investments reflect the communication and culture of the organization?

- *Spiritual capital—Relationship capital* investments are important because the way people interact and communicate with each other, including customers, form the type of culture in an organization. When people are treated well they feel welcomed and when this behavior is passed on to others, a positive pattern is set. Alternatively, uncaring, negative behavior will poison a work environment and strain relationships that customers will perceive.

Resiliency and Sustainability

What investments support an organization's ability to withstand difficult times?

- *Relationship capital—Spiritual capital* investments are important links between intangible and tangible investments. Internal team exercises to build a culture of cooperation, sharing, and congeniality creates a work environment that honors people. This, in turn, generates goodwill and a willingness to go the extra mile for each other and the customer. Such a workplace creates satisfied employees and a greater willingness to work hard for the company.

• *Human capital—Spiritual capital* investments are investments that create critically humane norms within entities that comfort and support the spiritual side of work. Building a culture of caring and support, in turn, grows the intestinal fortitude needed when times are tough. Because employees know the company cares, they will be more understanding when difficult decisions are made that negatively affect their time or salaries.

• *Customer capital—Organizational capital* investments support the strategies and tactics needed to guide a business in a defined direction that minimizes confusion. The customer's needs and expectations keep a business focused and the organization's processes and procedures keep the operations on a proven course.

Creativity and Innovation

What investments are critical to supporting a competitive edge (of products and services) that builds intellectual capital?

- *Human capital—Customer capital* investments are important because without understanding what is needed by, or of concern to users, one cannot optimize the desirability of products and services.

- *Relationship capital—Customer capital* investments seek to value the customer beyond seeing customers as buyers of goods and services. Investing in efforts to build team relationships and collaboration with customers generates new ideas for products and services and, as a result, value. Support of both forms of capital increases the potential for high ROI, as they serve to facilitate subsequent task-side investments as well.

- *Human capital—Spiritual capital* investments are often overlooked. Why work on building morale or a desirable workplace beyond the basics? Competitors! Some of the most creative and desirable workplaces are fun places, supporting the non-work side of employees' lives. Google, Apple, and other technology companies have built multiple refreshing distractions to help employees find ways in the workplace to step away from the work while *at* work. The benefits are clear—reinvigorated thinking, invigorated social interactions, more ideas from informal conversations with colleagues, and greater creativity and innovation.

Intellectual Property and Corporate Memory

What investments generate great value and protect the enterprise?

- *Human capital—Organizational capital* investments are important because people are most associated with the production of new processes, procedures, and inventions. By investing in people and their creative potential, more output is possible for producing intellectual properties and proprietary methods. This investment is critical as a means to capture the knowledge of the business. This is the focal point of Knowledge Management. In today's knowledge-driven economy, corporate memory is the jewel that needs to be polished and protected.

Tangible Drivers of Products and Services

What investments are important in producing new products and services?

- *Financial capital* is the banker for a business enterprise. It is the one investment that flows through every other investment. In a real way, it is the lifeblood of the enterprise. Support people and they will help build the business.

- *Financial capital—Human capital* investments are fundamental for a successful enterprise. People ultimately create the intellectual capital which generates value for the business. It is important to make certain that they are funded to keep up their expertise.

- *Financial capital—Relationship capital* investments are fundamental in building a team culture.

- *Financial capital—Spiritual capital* investments are fundamental in creating a desirable workplace that cares about its people.

- *Financial capital—Customer capital* investments are fundamental in learning whether products and services address the needs of the buyers. Interfacing with customers accelerates moving products and services to market.

- *Financial capital—Physical capital* investments are fundamental in supporting the efforts of the people in the business. Add technology that enhances results or simplifies work or creates new products, plus train people, and they will accelerate the ability to build IC and value.

- *Financial capital—Organizational capital* investments are fundamental in building the business and protecting corporate knowledge. Funding these investments provides the energy for creativity and innovation, the source of new intellectual capital.

....

Combining investments multiplies financial and competitive gains in a business.

....

CHAPTER 8

TREASURE HUNT: FINDING BURIED TREASURE IN YOUR ENTERPRISE

As noted in the prior chapters, there is much more value in an organization than can be found on financial ledgers. Since using tables and graphics helps me think and see more clearly, I have provided Figure 1. It reinforces the interactions that create value we described in the previous chapter by visually connecting M-7 investments with each other. I also added bullets for the investments to help recall what each one covers. This figure is effectively an overview of the M-7 investments. The task-side investments are shaded and the people side ones are not. Since 71 percent of value in an enterprise is derived from people, buried treasure is found in leveraging the talents and experiences of people.

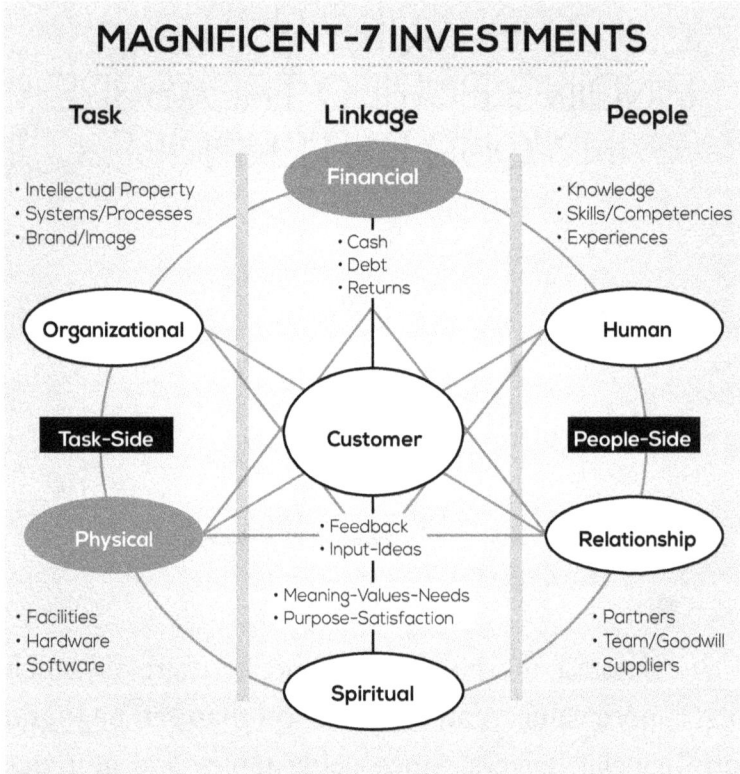

MAGNIFICENT-7 INVESTMENTS

Task · Linkage · People

- Intellectual Property
- Systems/Processes
- Brand/Image

Financial
- Cash
- Debt
- Returns

- Knowledge
- Skills/Competencies
- Experiences

Organizational · Human

Task-Side · Customer · People-Side

Physical · Relationship

- Feedback
- Input-Ideas

- Facilities
- Hardware
- Software

- Meaning-Values-Needs
- Purpose-Satisfaction

- Partners
- Team/Goodwill
- Suppliers

Spiritual

©1994-2017 Baldwin H. Tom

FIGURE 1. The Interactivity of M-7 Investments

Intellectual Capital–The Basis of Wealth

Since Intellectual Capital (IC) includes all the people-side investments, along with people-derived organization capital, and is the source of a great deal of intangible value generation within an organization, it makes sense to focus on people to build wealth in the enterprise. It is no longer in doubt: people are our greatest assets.

Seeking Talent for Intellectual Capital and High Value

The book *Talent Valuation*[10] by McGuire and Brenner not only provides an algorithm to measure IC but also provides a framework that links talent directly to shareholder valuation. The authors provide a rethinking of the entire human resource (HR) function, from the role of talent to new responsibilities of the HR executive. Recognizing that talented people are the focal points in creating value and wealth in organizations, they make the point that if maximal value is the goal, a business needs to fully support top talent to generate IC. There are two approaches to achieve this—build talent from within or buy talent from without. In the former, equity finances the talent acquisition, while in the latter, the business uses debt financing. Do you want to grow more top talent or buy it? Growing is a strategic approach and buying is a tactical one, with the expectation that buying a star now will add value immediately. This is the same thinking commonly employed in the professional sports world—it is what coaches do when they draft football players. Do they want a proven star now, or

---

[10] McGuire, Thomas, and Linda Brenner. *Talent Valuation: Accelerate Market Capitalization through Your Most Important Asset*. Pearson Education Ltd., 2015.

to invest time grooming a young player to become a future star?

Continuing with the sports analogy, HR must always be looking for top talent. HR needs to understand where top talent is needed within an organization because not all positions are equal in terms of direct impact on ROI. Clearly, HR needs to view personnel differently. Are vacant positions essential to value production? If so, they need to be supported well. This talent-driven culture of value creation builds a success-oriented brand for the enterprise. With this rethinking of the HR function, it should become clear that HR must perform more as the economic driver of the enterprise and less as personnel support. To uncover all the treasure buried in the business enterprise, the HR professional needs to have authority as an equal partner in the executive suite of the business.

M-7 in the Marketplace

To appreciate the importance of M-7 investments, one only has to consider the loss of valuation of a merger when two companies, with perfect task-side complementarity, unravel. Why? Their two cultures clashed. Relationships (chemistries and team synergies) that existed and worked well in each company were eliminated by the merger. The spiritual capital on both sides was ignored and thus destroyed. The merger focused on the tangible-side investments, such as physical and financial assets. The value of tangible assets is easier to appreciate and be recognized because traditional *capital investments* refer to this component. We discuss M-7 in the context of mergers next.

As people are undoubtedly the most valuable asset in a business, it follows that the human resource function is a key economic engine.

CHAPTER 9

M-7 IN PRACTICE– MERGERS & ACQUISITIONS

A s will be seen in the following discussion of Mergers & Acquisitions (M&A), the failure to understand the tremendous leverage potential of judicious investments can result in significant monetary loss or even loss of the entire business enterprise.

The Cost of Not Leveraging Your Greatest Untapped Assets

In every enterprise, the goal is to provide services and products with an expected positive ROI from tangible (e.g., funds and things) and intangible inputs (e.g., people power, sweat). In seeking high returns, or maximal value, leaders must invest effectively in the effort; investments are a solution to solving a problem. There are two types of resources that may be used to generate returns—things and people. And there is a cost in not leveraging your greatest asset—people— and what they contribute.

Corporate Mergers and Acquisitions as a Test of M-7

As M&A are investments, these are useful examples to test the value of effective investing in M-7 to show successes and failures. Even more important is to not appreciate existing investments within the merging entities.

To illustrate the usefulness of the M-7 framework, I reviewed the M&A in the corporate, health care, and accounting settings to further explore M-7 investments.

M&A transactions are not for the faint of heart. The allure of fast-tracking acquisitions of a new business, new customers, or new ideas for a business propels executive teams to seek M&As, even with statistics that say that most M&A efforts fail. By one account, only 50 percent succeed.[11] A more dire statistic says

---

[11] Forbes Leadership Forum. "Why Half of All M&A Deals Fail, and What You Can Do About It." *Forbes*. October 09, 2014. https://www.forbes.com/sites/forbesleadershipforum/2012/03/19/why-half-of-all-ma-deals-fail-and-what-you-

that between 70-90 percent fail.[12] The consensus of consultants and those who evaluate merger failures is that cultural incompatibilities cause 67 percent of M&A fatalities. No question, mergers are risky. Yet the potential to win attracts executives to bet on success. A successful merger can catapult a good business into an exceptional one.

When viewed as two bodies merging, it becomes clear that there are many moving parts and differences that have to be integrated in a merger. With this visual analogy in mind, it is expected that there may be many different reasons why a merger fails or succeeds. Our goal is not to study M&A to analyze their successes and failures, but to determine what role M-7 plays in M&As. The M-7 investments are like nerves in the body. They activate and manipulate different parts of the enterprise. Linked together with strategies, goals, and needs, the body can move toward a successful integration.

As one should expect, with the meager success rate of mergers, there are many consultants with answers about how to design and implement a successful merger. Here is a compiled list of suggestions from corporate consultants to improve M&A success. We have captured and categorized these suggestions under M-7 investment categories.

can-do-about-it/.

[12] Christensen, Clayton M., Richard Alton, Curtis Rising, and Andrew Waldeck. "The Big Idea: The New M&A Playbook." *Harvard Business Review,* March 2011

- Spiritual capital/Relationship capital (culture)
  - Assess and reinforce cultural compatibility (alignment) of people, operational, and financial areas
- Human capital
  - Maintain depth of bench and resources with managerial bandwidth
  - Build a M&A leadership team
- Customer capital
  - Ensure customer match, including customer profile and target market
- Financial capital
  - Match financials (revenues, conversion rate, burn rate, margins) of merging entities
- Operational/spiritual/relationship/human capitals (processes, strategies, tactics)
  - Complete, robust due diligence before a merger—sorting implications and alternatives
  - Establish integration and communications plan to minimize surprises
  - Anticipate emergent business model post-merger

- Align corporate strategies and business goals

- Build resiliency of merging entities to withstand unexpected challenges

Even with advance warning, mergers often move forward and get into trouble. I suggest that beyond ignorance on the part of the executive team, another reason is that M&As are of maximal complexity, which leads to the most common reasons why mergers, even when they address consultants' suggestions, frequently fail to live up to expectations:

- Management issues
  - Arrogance of leadership; not listening to warnings
  - Poor time management needed to carefully address issues; rushing decisions

- Cultural issues
  - Not addressing all the cultural aspects, especially those that generated chemistry and creative leveraging within each merging entity; losing interactions that generate value and wealth

- Environmental issues
  - Not understanding the merged entity and

its place in the new business environment;
missing clues for effective decision-making

• Unexpected issues

– Problems resulting from poor due diligence, neglecting the intangible cultures
that facilitate creativity, innovation, and
value generation

– Loss of key member(s) of merging teams

A merged entity is like a puzzle piece with multiple
connectors that need to lock into complementary
connectors in the new (post-merger), robust
environment and its customers. The challenge is to
find the proper fit to optimize a ROI. The integrators
of the newly merged entity have the responsibility
to maximize connections to the new environment
and new customers. This just adds another layer of
difficulty to guarantee merger success, which means
that anticipating and planning for post-merger
integration is possibly more important than the more
exciting preplanning stage and the merger itself.

Failed Corporate Mergers

There are always lessons to be learned from failures—
probably more than from successes. Let us review some
high-profile merger failures in the corporate world.

We have learned that while investments (applied or

not) play important roles, success also needs good leadership and management to leverage merger positives and to embrace merger opportunities in a timely way.

Arby's and Wendy's (Three Years, $2 billion loss)

In 2008, the owner of fast-food chain Arby's bought burger chain Wendy's for $2.34 billion, hoping to bolster Arby's fortunes with an infusion from much larger Wendy's. Once the assets of the two businesses were combined, Wendy's generated 70 percent of the revenues. Wendy's continued to improve product offerings, while Arby's languished over the next few years, well into 2010. Additionally, the merger eroded Wendy's value as it declined due to the merger. The combined group ultimately decided to sell 81.5 percent of Arby's to a private equity group for $430 million after the roast-beef sandwich chain continually struggled to grow its profits, retaining the Wendy's brand. Arby's was sold in June 2011. This was not a true merger; it was an acquisition, as both entities maintained their identities and business lines. But it was most definitely a failure as an integration of two businesses. Since this was not a traditional merger of two businesses but more a merger of two business offices, i.e., a financial transaction, the M-7 investments that were in play focused on financial and physical. One might suggest that the main cause for failure was that there was little or no synergy created by the effort. Clearly, the people-side investments were not addressed, except the customer capital efforts. If customers purchasing meals is the key factor for success, then we might suggest that investments in customer capital were flawed on Arby's side that led to the financial drag on the merged entity.

Sprint and Nextel (Eight Years, $36 Billion Loss)

In 2005, when the merger of two cellular giants was accepted by both Sprint and Nextel, it was considered by many as a $36 billion merger of equals. Disagreements started almost immediately. Initially, Nextel designed a merged logo with Nextel at the front. Sprint came back with another logo, with Nextel the minority player. There did not appear to be any coordination from the beginning, and this dissonance was accentuated by each entity maintaining its respective headquarters. This was confusing for customers but reinforced the very different cultures trying to merge, which were extremely different—Nextel's was aggressive and entrepreneurial, while Sprint's was fully bureaucratic, with delineated chains of command. Operationally, Sprint's customer service was poor, while Nextel was tuned into their customers. Additionally, the two enterprises' technologies proved to be a challenge to align as well. Both companies recognized this and sought consultants and teams to try to merge the

Sprint-Nextel disparity. Unfortunately, it was not enough. Along with a great deal of mistrust among the two entities' leaders, the clash of cultures led to a large-scale exit of Nextel executives.

In three years (2008) Sprint had written off $30 billion. By the time Sprint finally pulled the plug on the deal in 2013, Nextel's entire $36 billion valuation was gone. As Sprint closed down Nextel, less than half of those customers rejoined the Sprint service. Clearly, all the people-side investments took a hit here. Specifically, relationships between Sprint and Nextel were never built, customer capital was not fostered, spiritual capital was destroyed, and human capital seemed neglected. When we say 71% of an enterprise is impacted by people-side investments, this case suggests that these executives were oblivious to that fact!

AOL and Time Warner (Six Years, $66 Billion Loss)
It is understandable why the AOL-Time Warner merger has become a case study at business schools. The merger had every aspect of flawed execution and unfortunate circumstances from start to finish. It has been called "the worst merger in history" and "a colossal mistake." The factors involved in this legendary disaster include the board, executives, leadership, due diligence, staff/employees, customers, the political and financial environment, infighting,

and intractable cultural incompatibility. As a means to understand the M-7 investment implications of this merger, I have reframed the merger stages based on an excellent *New York Times* postmortem of the merger by Tim Arango.[13]

Understanding the Opportunity

A 2010 survey by McKinsey & Company found that nearly 70 percent of mergers in their database failed to achieve the revenue synergies expected by the management. Companies try mergers in order to accelerate moving into new markets, gaining new technologies, or reaching new client populations. No executive enters into a merger expecting to fail; yet, if they continue to follow the same practices of the past, most will fail.

In 2000, AOL (to gain content and cable networks) announced that it was buying Time Warner (to gain internet presence) for $160 billion to create, as CNET. com said, the "world's largest media company." Bringing together the leading Internet company with the leading media company to create an entity that would be the leaders in the new century was an exciting undertaking. The print media spoke of the potential for the merger as transformative. There were

---

[13] Arango, Tim. "How the AOL-Time Warner Merger Went So Wrong." *The New York Times*, The New York Times, 10 Jan. 2010, www.nytimes.com/2010/01/11/business/media/11merger.html.

few critics, although the regulators at the Federal Trade Commission did not believe the merger made financial sense.

Framing the Opportunity

Most everyone expected the AOL/Time Warner merger to succeed. Wall Street analysts were high on their prospects for success. With seasoned executives running the show, the opportunity seemed too good to fail. During the postmortem, it became clear that many of the actions that were needed to ensure a successful integration were not taken, or were executed poorly. Each of the factors listed below is grist for lengthy discussions.

Before the Merger

- Incomplete due diligence evaluating organizational capabilities

- Board and cultural differences

After the Merger

- Expected post-merger synergies between the two companies were affected by external circumstances, like the 9/11 terrorist attacks on New York City and Washington, DC

- Superficial merger occurred at the corporate level only

- Resentment between each company's employees

- Unstable corporate structure as both partners feuded over CFO position, with four different CFOs in the first three years

- Resignation of Time Warner's CEO only one year into the merger

- Inadequate execution to integrate the two companies

- Lack of collaboration within the merged company, with resistance to implement growth strategies that accentuated a lack of direction

Cultural Situation in the Merged Company

The merger should have worked but did not. Why? The simple answer is that their cultures clashed. Interestingly, one might expect from their due diligence that the two teams knew what they were getting into and what needed to be addressed for merger success. Another way to say this is that, while the due diligence was on target, the post-merger social integration was flawed. After all, getting people to work together to talk to each other and to solve problems is critical in navigating necessary cultural integration. The human factor played a dominant role here. When executives could not agree, disagreements and animosities spilled into the workforce, causing staff to see each other as adversaries rather than teammates. Indeed, it was said that both teams seemed to hate each other. Moving forward with integration in these circumstances became strained and very difficult. There was little leveraging of collective *smarts*, where $1+1 = 2$, and not 7.

Lesson learned? Culture is much more complex than is obvious, and the merged entity revealed layers of complexity of culture that were not obvious in the premerger due diligence.

Execution Issues for the Merged Company

The challenge extended beyond cultural alignment to systems, processes, and customer alignment as well. How, who, what, when, and where needed to be answered for all aspects that required alignment. Postmerger stabilization just got more complicated. Aligning different cultures, organization systems, and business models makes execution of postmerger integration very complex. Clearly, this was a strategic, not a tactical effort to sort the nuances of the complexities in the Time Warner-AOL case. Arango effectively suggested that if the two companies' leadership viewed the merger as an event and not a process, they were doomed to fail. When a merger is considered an event, then the work is done once papers are signed. When viewed as a process, by way of contrast, once the papers are signed, the hard work begins.

Just three years after the merger, by 2003, Time Warner dropped AOL from its official name. In another three years, in 2006, Time Warner separated entirely from AOL. Jerry Levin, who sold Time Warner to AOL, later told CNBC, "I presided over the worst deal of the century, apparently." The result? After six years and a $99 billion write-off, the deal realized a $66 billion loss from the original $160 billion sale and a failed merger. This figure does not include the devastation to families from job and retirement account losses, nor its impact on customers.

It appears from the aftermath of this merger that the executives missed considering the long-term strategic efforts needed to consolidate the merger. They missed understanding the ongoing, continuous process of change needed to deliver on the merger's promised returns. Arango concludes his analysis with missed opportunities for key actions in a successful merger:

1. Cost savings have to be generated.

2. Leaders need to be appointed and gain the trust and confidence of those who must follow them.

3. Technical processes and IT systems must be melded together seamlessly.

4. Customers and other stakeholders need to receive communications to help them understand how to interact with the new combined organization.

5. Duplicate sales forces have to be consolidated without disrupting customer relationships.

6. A single culture must be created that welcomes each person's contributions regardless of previous loyalties.

7. Boards of directors may need to be consolidated.

More Lessons Learned and M-7 Investment

There are layers of activities focused on Intellectual Capital in play here. It starts with investing effort in human capital (staff mergers, people staying and working together), relationship capital (board and leadership alignment), and spiritual capital (morale, culture). Beyond this set is organizational capital (processes, procedures), plus an overlay of customer capital. Understanding these diverse moving parts has to be part of the strategic planning to integrate the two companies into a new, smooth-running enterprise. Recognizing the significant change of these areas and the need for implementing change management strategies is critical for M&A success.

There is more to this endeavor than knowing what needs to be done. It is also about stamina, perseverance to stay the course to the finish, and knowing how to not disrupt ongoing business while chaotic change is occurring. Keeping all the balls in the air requires a dedicated, well-organized team. Yet overall, nearly two-thirds of business combinations still fail, mostly because leaders are not fully prepared to handle the complex, continuous change that mergers and acquisitions involve. In the next section, we consider health care mergers and the lessons they provide.

Health Care Dynamics

The health care industry is in flux today because federal government mandates are pressing the industry to move from a fee-for-service (volume-based) culture to a value-based one. This calls for significant change and places performance pressure on the industry. On top of economic and tactical changes driven by the Patient Protection and Affordable Care Act of 2010 and the continuing need to compete for patients and business, this industry is in the midst of both strategic and structural change. The incentives for mergers thus center on the need to survive and compete in an uncertain market.

M-7 and Recommendations for Health Care Mergers
I reviewed eleven sets of recommendations and commentaries for merger success and trends in the health care area and extrapolated the different M-7 investments that were considered in each. The health care recommendations and associated M-7 investments are tabulated in Table 4, with summaries following the table. The eleven investments show that relational and financial capital, followed by human and organizational capital, are mentioned most. As a group, all investments are considered equally important here in the recommendations, except physical capital. This is shown in the M-7 Totals column in Table 4.

TABLE 4 **M-7 Recommendations via Consultants***

M-7 Investment	#1	#2	#3	#4	#5	#6	#7	#8	#9	#10	#11	M-7 Totals
1. Human Capital	x		x	x	x		x	x	x		x	8
2. Relationship Capital	x		x	x		x	x	x	x	x	x	9
3. Financial Capital		x	x	x	x	x		x	x	x	x	9
4. Customer Capital			x	x	x	x	x	x			x	7
5. Spiritual Capital	x	x	x	x	x		x	x				7
6. Organizational Capital	x		x	x	x		x	x	x	x		8
7. Physical Capital		x						x	x			3
TOTALS	4	3	6	6	5	3	5	7	5	3	4	

*Sources used to populate Table 4 follow.

1. **Three Prescriptions for Successful Healthcare Mergers[14]**

    The Affordable Care Act requirements to improve care while reducing costs have spurred an increase of M&A activity. Many health care organizations consider mergers and acquisitions as a solution to spread cost and improve care. But many M&A attempts fail. Here are three strategies that should improve the success rate: Strategy 1: Communicate early and often to establish expectations, strengthen relationships, and build confidence during uncertain times. Strategy 2: Integrate local cultures to understand how each company does business. Strategy 3: Structure an approach to managing change that offsets inevitable disruptions from a merger that includes integrating cultures and improves outcomes.

2. **Key Tips for a Successful Hospital Merger or Acquisition[15]**

    The health care regulatory framework and new federal guidelines have fostered a national trend toward consolidation to achieve economies of scale and boost profitability. "There are many variables and catalysts influencing the systemic change that

---

[14] Gallup, Inc. "Three Prescriptions for Successful Healthcare Mergers." Gallup. com, 19 Nov. 2014, www.gallup.com/businessjournal/179486/three-prescriptions-successful-healthcare-mergers.aspx.

[15] Schmidt, Peter J. "Key Tips for a Successful Hospital Merger or Acquisition." *Healthcare Finance News*, 2 July 2015, www.healthcarefinancenews.com/blog/key-tips-successful-hospital-merger-or-acquisition.

is underway in the hospital sector. Given the need for capital, heavy regulatory burdens, and changing models of reimbursement, independent hospitals are increasingly turning to mergers and acquisitions as a means to address the business and financial challenges they face. Through careful planning, thorough due diligence, and strategic integration posttransaction, hospitals can join forces to meet the challenges they face and succeed in today's ever-changing health care marketplace."

3. **Top 10 Pivotal Factors for Successful Mergers and Acquisitions[16]**

The shift to value-based care is driving the need to join forces to survive the dramatically shifting ground for health care providers. The article focuses on mission, timing, market, customer base, organization goals, culture alignment, buy-in of stakeholders, partner alignment for efficiencies, determining the merged future, and achieving gains expected from merger.

4. **9 Ways to Help Make Health Care Provider M&As Successful[17]**

As more and more providers work to find ways

---

[16] Valentine, Steven, and Daniel Juberg. "Top 10 Pivotal Factors for Successful Mergers and Acquisitions." *GE Healthcare Camden Group*, Oct. 2015, www.thecamdengroup.com/thought-leadership/top-ten/top-10-pivotal-factors-for-successful-mergers-and-acquisitions/.

[17] Tsokanos, Jim. "9 Ways to Help Make Health Care Provider M&As Successful." *Jim Tsokanos.net*, 29 Nov. 2016, jimtsokanos.net/9-ways-help-make-healthcare-provider-mas-successful/.

of navigating tough economic realities and the ongoing pressure of health care reform, they should consider nine factors: (1) mission clarity, (2) timing of merger, (3) market and share, (4) size to expand, (5) structure, (6) culture alignment, (7) stakeholder support, (8) due diligence for efficiencies, and (9) business plan of operational efficiencies.

5. **8 Trends in Healthcare Mergers & Acquisitions for 2017**[18]

These are trends and not recommendations for M&A success. However, they provide a sense of what the 450 surveyed executives think about the health care environment. Of these, 31 percent will launch new product lines, up from 17 percent in 2016 (competitive strategies and tactics); 38 percent said M&A driving growth plans versus 41 percent in 2016 (M&A still important); 26 percent of those using M&A said that organic growth is their top strategy (strengthening value ahead of mergers); almost half of respondents said capital needs will rise in 2017 and 42 percent expect further increases in the year ahead; only 25 percent said this in 2016; 59 percent (versus 33 percent in 2016) said the Affordable Care Act is their chief concern in

[18] Dyrda, Laura. "8 Trends in Healthcare Mergers & Acquisitions for 2017." *Becker's ASC Review*, 10 Jan. 2017, www.beckersasc.com/asc-transactions-and-valuation-issues/8-trends-in-healthcare-mergers-acquisitions-for-2017.html.

2017 (dealing with value-based care requirements from volume-based still challenging); 18 percent said regulatory uncertainty was their top challenge for 2017, while 33 percent said so in 2016 (there seems greater clarity around regulations now); 94 percent said their business's financial performance will be on par or better than it was in 2016; 61 percent anticipate a better year in 2017 than 2016 (optimism).

6. **Report: 3 Key Healthcare Merger and Acquisition Trends[19]**

Health care organizations are positioning themselves for value-based, at-risk reimbursements. The trends here include: 1) Risks moving forward require strategic thinking and transactions and understanding where the market will go. 2) Look to non-ownership collaborations instead of mergers. [Combine without giving up ownership.] 3) Increase in nonprofit mergers.

7. **Salesforce Integration Generates M&A Success in Healthcare[20]**

This article notes that salesforce integration is the key to merger success with two large health care

[19] Adamopoulos, Helen. "Report: 3 Key Healthcare Merger and Acquisition Trends." *Becker's Hospital Review*, 21 Nov. 2013, www.beckershospitalreview.com/hospital-transactions-and-valuation/report-3-key-healthcare-merger-and-acquisition-trends.html.

[20] "Salesforce Integration Generates M&A Success in Healthcare." Bain & Company. June 2017. http://www.bain.com/about/client-results/salesforce-integration-generates-m-and-a-success-in-healthcare.aspx.

companies. Bain consultants developed a strategy and plan. They effectively merged two salesforces with different sales cultures. Bain identified the desired end-state outcome, characterized the current state, engaged leadership, and set up a well-documented implementation program while working closely with the teams.

8. **Biotech and Big Pharma: Keys to a Successful M&A**[21]
This article focuses on biotech and pharmaceutical merger considerations: (1) research collaboration; (2) clarity on goals; (3) culture compatibility; (4) values alignment; (5) conversations; communication and education; (6) no assumptions, (7) value creation—where and how, (8) no matter what, "it's going to be messy," (9) discipline—go slow before going fast during integration; (10) silos require bridges; (11) transparent communications and relationship-building; (12) value creation *not* by cutting and synergizing, but by translating existing successful practices. This means it is better not to totally absorb a smaller biotech entity into a larger pharmaceutical and lose the value creation functions. It's more about building growth platforms.

---

[21] "Biotech and Big Pharma: Keys to a Successful M&A." *FTI Journal*. January 2016. http://www.ftijournal.com/article/biotech-and-big-pharma-keys-to-a-successful-m-and-a.

9. 7 Issues Healthcare CEOs Should Consider Before Engaging in M&A[22]

Careful preparation by the CEO is the foundation for a successful health care M&A. (1) Understand and consider trends around your verticals that may often change, e.g., in medical equipment. (2) Have a vision to guide target for merger, so the end result is aligned with desired direction of business. (3) Create a detailed checklist for due diligence with input from all functional areas. (4) Postacquisition and merger integration process must be led by an experienced team. The key is that integration process is central to a merger, not an afterthought, because understanding the integration effort brings financial and operational reality to the effort. (5) Funding the merger needs to be considered early. What are the financing sources and working capital needs? (6) Anticipating and planning for the inevitable breakdowns protects the merger team from "OMG" moments. (7) Engage experts and consultants early in the process to be part of teams to minimize risks that will arise in the merger process.

[22] Schramski, Tom. "7 Issues Healthcare CEOs Should Consider Before Engaging in M&A." *Axial Forum.* May 10, 2016. http://www.axial.net/forum/7-issues-healthcarehealthcare-ceos-consider-engaging-ma/.

10. What Hospital Executives Should be Considering in Hospital Mergers and Acquisitions[23]

The health care market is experiencing unprecedented change. Strategic, economic, and regulatory pressures are causing hospitals and health systems to consider integration and consolidation. In this white paper, the authors point out the five types of transactions with their advantages and disadvantages: (1) Affiliations, (2) Joint Ventures, (3) Joint Operating Agreement, (4) Merger, and (5) Acquisition. Reasons to seek a transaction include seeking economies of scale, adding clinical or managerial strengths, and gaining geographical reach. They suggest a three-phase disciplined approach in transactions: (1) Discovery phase—learn all you can and then decide whether to proceed or not; (2) Design phase—which partner, governance, projections, joint vision, and (3) Deployment phase—establish the new entity's governance, accountability plans, operational and process development.

11. Looking at Hospital M&A Activity in the Value-Based Care World[24]

Hospitals and health systems are seeking capabilities

---

[23] Yanci, Jim, Michael Wolford, and Paige Young. "What Hospital Executives Should Be Considering in Hospital Mergers and Acquisitions." Dixon Hughes Goodman. 2013. Accessed September 21, 2017. http://www2.dhgllp.com/res_pubs/Hospital-Mergers-and-Acquisitions.pdf.

[24] Landi, Heather. "Looking at Hospital M&A Activity in the Value-Based Care World." *Healthcare Informatics Magazine.* November 11, 2016. https://www.healthcare-informatics.com/article/payment/looking-hospital-ma-activity-value-based-care-world.

for value-based health care through M&A. These capabilities include acquiring health IT, technology, and data analytics. More than 100 transactions took place in 2016, with four drivers: (1) smaller organizations under financial or clinical distress; (2) community-based hospitals partnering for intellectual or financial capacity to be more value-based health care providers; (3) players who felt the need for partners to reduce their cost structure to compete; and (4) large, multihospital systems adjusting to markets. There are important factors needed in a merger to sustain a successful value-based operation: clinical and physician alignment; quality and safety; care management capability; clinical and business intelligence; networked development configuration; financial strength; purchaser relationships; customer service and engagement; and finally, leadership and governance. The health care industry is in flux, with innovative structures and ideas being tested, like the use of video for virtual visits and consultations. Who will control the dollar—physicians, hospitals, insurers? It is yet uncertain what the health care company of the future might look like and how it will provide services.

My birds-eye view tells me the following. Everything is in flux due to the new strategic, economic, and regulatory drivers forcing the need for change. I agree with the "Biotech and Big Pharma" panel, who said no matter how one looks at the health care area, "It's going to be messy." Thus, financial focus is critical to remain vital while addressing the need to move from a fee-based to a value-based culture in health care. This is good for the customer, but a major headache for health care executives, who are searching for funds for infrastructural changes to buy new equipment, new technology, new billing systems, new databases, and even new locations. Beyond these financial and physical needs, there is also the need to align doctors and staff to this new way of doing business.

Even though consultants universally recommend the importance of the intangible investments in a merger, and that cultural integration is an important post-merger concern, as most (67 percent) health care executives agree, more than half still say their failure to merge cultural differences cost them value from a merger. This means *culture* is much more complex than first understood—a theme already seen with the corporate mergers.

As we review M&A in accounting firms, will we see the same challenges with culture?

Accounting Firm Mergers and M-7 Investments

Today's Big Four accounting firms were formed

through M&As; the Big Four used to be the Big Eight. But mergers in 1989 reduced the Big Eight to Big Six. Then, in 1996, the Big Six was reduced to the Big Five. In 2002, when Arthur Anderson was dropped because of its participation in the Enron scandal, the Big Five became the Big Four.[25]

The following are the four largest firms in the world today. They provide massive employment and career development opportunities to accountants and auditors around the world.[26]

1. **Deloitte** was founded in 1845, and through a series of mergers and reorganizations, is now the largest among the Big Four. In 2016, it earned $36.8 billion and had 244,400 employees in more than 150 countries.

2. **Pricewaterhouse Coopers (PwC):** In 2016, the firm earned $35.9 billion, with 223,400 employees in 157 countries. PwC was formed from the 1998 merger of Price Waterhouse and Coopers & Lybrand.

3. **Ernst & Young:** Formed from a merger

---

[25] Wootton, Charles W., and Carel M. Wolk. "The Development of 'The Big Eight' Accounting Firms in the United States, 1900 to 1990." *Accounting Historians Journal.* Accessed September 21, 2017. http://www.accountingin.com/accounting-historians-journal/volume-19-number-1/the-development-of-the-big-eight-accounting-firms-in-the-united-states-1900-to-1990/.

[26] "Big 4 Accounting Firms - Who They Are, Facts and Information." *Accountingverse.com.* Accessed September 21, 2017. http://www.accountingverse.com/articles/big-4-accounting-firms.html.

in 1989 of Ernst & Whinney with Arthur Young, in 2016, the company's revenues were $29.6 billion, with 231,000 employees in 150 countries.

4. **Klynveld Peat Marwick Goerdeler (KPMG):** KPMG resulted from the 1987 merger of Peat Marwick International with Klynveld Main Goerdeler. In 2016, revenues were $25.4 billion with 189,000 staff in 155 countries.

Accounting Culture

According to Joel Sinkin and Terrence Putney, accounting firms all have common features, yet it is in the culture that one finds distinct differences.[27] The common features include (1) their total focus on accuracy of numbers, (2) their yearly dedicated time for tax and audit work from January through April 15 (the American Internal Revenue Service tax deadline), and (3) the traditional bureaucratic corporate-ladder-climbing approach to getting ahead.

With these common denominators, one might expect an easy path to mergers. As it turns out, however, just as in other industries, accounting mergers succeed because of culture fit and fail because of culture misalignments. Poor alignments lead to both staff and client turnover,

---

[27] Sinkin, Joel, and Terrence Putney. "The Culture Test." *Journal of Accountancy*. May 01, 2014. https://www.journalofaccountancy.com/issues/2014/may/20139298.html.

a very undesirable outcome for accounting practices. Sinkin and Putney point out the difficulties and complexities of culture with accounting firms. They make the point that carefully defining premerger cultures and assessing their importance is the key to success. They break *culture* into three categories:

1. **Organizational culture:** This encompasses *work ethic* (hours of work), *policies and procedures* (value system and management style), and *team versus individual* efforts. These three aspects fall under Spiritual Capital in the M-7 schema.

2. **Client services culture:** This category fits broadly under Customer Capital in M-7. Separately, Sinkin and Putney note billing procedures (fixed or hourly rates) as part of this aspect of culture, or Financial Capital in M-7. They group *client demographics* (types, size, industry, and services), *staff leverage* (owner to nonowner ratios), and number of *specialists and generalists* in a practice together. These latter three fit under Human Capital in M-7.

3. **Owner issues culture:** Sinkin and Putney refer to owner's compensation (formulae, performance evaluation), owner's agreement

(compensation, retirement, taking clients), and compensation level and range. All of these are part of Financial Capital in M-7.

Research specialist and financial writer Mary Ellen Biery refers to key merger factors according to Phillip J. Whitman (President and CEO of Whitman Business Advisors LLC) as compensation and governance.[28] While these are broken out differently, they are all part of what others define as culture of the firm. Again, it is culture in its broadest sense that will make or break a deal.

Thus, success in a merger according to Whitman includes how merging partners complement or overlap client bases (customer capital); what sets them apart or their areas of specialization (human/organizational capital); the chemistry between managing partners (human/spiritual capital); and their respective cultures—e.g., ideas, customs, skill, arts, etc. that are transferred, communicated, or passed along (spiritual capital).

As Biery says, "Culture affects strategic and operational priorities, like office décor." She effectively says that culture includes everything one does inside the walls of a business. Here are other aspects of culture:

---

[28] Biery, Mary Ellen Research Specialist. "7 Aspects of Your CPA Firm Culture That Can Make or Break a Merger." *Sageworks Blog.* July 14, 2014. https://www. sageworks.com/blog/post/2016/07/14/7-aspects-of-your-cpa-firm-culture-that-can-make-or-break-a-merger.aspx.

- Business development

- Defined internal norms of how superiors and partners are addressed

- Commitment to engage, develop, and retain high-potential talent

- Attitude toward leveraging staff

- Development of performance management culture

- Life/work balance

- Attitude toward technology

It is not surprising that, while most everyone understands that culture will make or break a deal, if due diligence is not performed carefully and one or more of these cultural factors is missed, it may well destroy a deal.

All Mergers Adhere to the 80/20 Principle

The Pareto Principle or 80/20 rule was coined by Joseph Juran in honor of Vilfredo Pareto who first wrote about it in the publication *Cours d'économie politique* (1896–97). Pareto was born in Paris but had dual citizenship with Italy. Pareto showed that 80 percent of the land in Italy was owned by 20 percent of the population. The 80/20 rule has been referred to in software (20 percent of the code creates 80 percent of the errors), sports (20 percent of the exercises provides 80 percent of the impact), occupational health (20 percent of the hazards accounts for 80 percent of the injuries), and wealth distribution (20 percent of the wealthiest individuals controls 80 percent of the world's income).

Regardless of the industry, all mergers follow a similar pattern. When all the aspects are charted, the similarities and differences fit the 80/20 rule, where 80 percent is similar, and only 20 percent is distinctive of a deal. Said differently, the outcome of a merger is controlled by only 20 percent of the activities. The first observation is that key investments in mergers, as illustrated in Figure 2, are on the Intellectual Capital side. The sizes of the circles imply emphases in a merger.

M-7 MERGER EMPHASIS

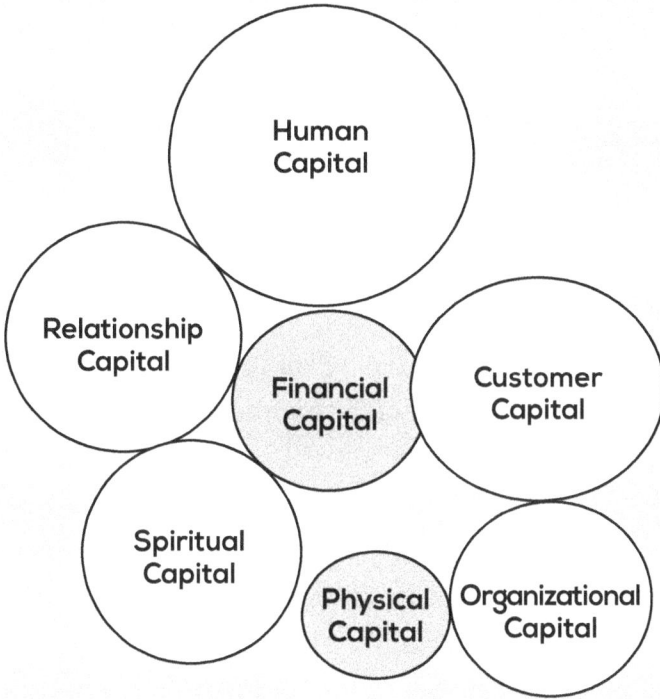

©1994-2017 Baldwin H. Tom

FIGURE 2. Key investments in Mergers Are in Intellectual Capital Components, Not in Financial or Physical Capital

In this review of M&As, I reviewed general Corporate (for-profit) businesses, health care, and Accounting firms to investigate investment differences among these industry groups. As a generalization, I suggest that 80 percent of the lessons and recommendations around mergers fit for all groups, summarized here and in Table 5.

- **Purpose.** While the purposes for M&A differ among industry groups, the key drivers tend to be very similar. For example, the reason firms seek to merge or acquire another company is to grow their customer base and increase revenues. Unique for the health care is financial survival because of new federal regulations that actually take money away for poor performance.

- **Drivers.** The desire for increasing revenues or containing losses are common among industry groups. There are differences regarding the reasons to broaden an organization's ability to reach new customers. On both the corporate and accounting sides, beating the competition is the important driver. At this time, the health care industry is focused on stemming losses from shrinking margins from penalties and the need to change structure to move from fee-based to value-based practices. There is an imperative for changing the business culture for health care.

- **Investments.** My goal in focusing on the M&A industry was to determine what M-7 investments might be involved in ways that decide the success or failure of a merger. Five of the seven capitals were identified as most important in mergers across the three examined industries. These five capitals encompass what have been defined as Intellectual Capital (IC). IC was the key, with five different capitals playing key roles, depending on the type of merger. This finding reinforces the fact that intangible assets are the most important, both in doing business and during efforts to merge with another business. In these transactions (Figure 2), focus on financial and physical capitals was less relevant. Future business financials need to reflect this.

• **Key Factor.** Understanding the complexity and nuances of culture before and after a merger has been the key challenge of all merger successes and failures. Understanding the long-term need to manage and to integrate cultural issues in the merged entity is critical to success. From our M-7 investment perspective, all the Intellectual Capital factors—human, relationship, customer, spiritual, and organizational investments—play important roles. While financial capital is important and may be the initiating factor for a merger, it plays a secondary role in the merged entity's success. Physical capital plays virtually no role in M&A success or failure except possibly in health care mergers, where serious restructuring is needed.

TABLE 5 Corporate, Health Care, and Accounting M&A

Topic	Corporate	Health Care	Accounting
Purpose for M&A	Growth, customers, new territory, revenues	Financial survival, penalty avoidance	New territory, compensation, governance, better fees
Key drivers for mergers	Loss of revenues; increase competitiveness to beat the competition; new products/ services	Strategic, economic, and regulatory changes; shrinking margins; regulatory penalties;	Competitive edge for clients and staff; new geography; new products/ services
Key M-7 Investments	Intellectual capital (first human, relationship, spiritual; then organizational and customer)	Financial first followed by physical; then human and other	Cultural (first human, customer, organizational, spiritual, then financial)
Key factor for merger success or failure	Culture alignment	Culture alignment	Culture alignment

Mergers and acquisitions provide fertile ground to study the roles of the investments in driving success or failure in these transactions.

CHAPTER 10

M-7 AS AN ORGANIZATION DIAGNOSTIC

All organizations function ideally when there are appropriate investments in people and tasks that produce exchanges of goods and services. When these exchanges take place, an enterprise thrives. Clearly value and business wealth (or loss of value) in an organization derives from these exchanges. It makes sense to consider using these M-7 investments as a diagnostic to assess an organization's health, as determined by its success in optimizing its M-7 investment portfolio.

Performance Metrics

Within the stages of moving from talent to value creation are multiple points for performance measure (metrics). The question is, which metric is most predictive of success, because not all measures are useful in valuing a business. These same points have the potential to become entries into the business's financials. In developing a diagnostic, it will be up to the executive team to determine which milestone or metric is key in measuring progress and success for a given time frame. In the examples below, I illustrate the use of the investments in conceptualizing the value optimization of a business.

M-7 Diagnostics and ROI

Figure 3 illustrates the concept that pairing investments helps to build value in an enterprise. In this example, human capital is paired with organizational capital to demonstrate how incremental investment in one capital is used to leverage a paired investment in the other. The customer (diagonal line) benefits from this set of investments. In this illustration, the investments produce increased value for the customer at each juncture. The Customer Capital line itself is drawn based on these increases. For example, if investment in the customer is to enhance customer participation and collaboration, a plan is developed to achieve those goals together with milestones. As each milestone is met as a result of relevant investments, the line is plotted as presented here. In our example, "data" is exploited via cell phones and personal computers; when staff are supported with Individual Development Plans (IDPs) to focus and support their efforts, the results lead to products and services for customers; as one moves to be more inclusive in an organization—department to division to organization—plus adds processes, systems, and enterprise tools of organizational capital to complement each, one gains value that accelerates customer capital.

In the management arena in the early 2000s, many technology-driven tools emerged to support the enterprise, from BPR (Business Process Reengineering) to LMS (Learning Management Systems) to ERP (Enterprise Resource Planning), all of which help make each of the areas covered more efficient and effective. These tools, when provided to trained personnel, help build value and wealth for the business.

In Figure 4, I have described some benefits to the customer from the incremental investments shown in Figure 3.

1. Investments in basic support to personnel with basic investment in organizational capital will provide *general products and services* to customers.

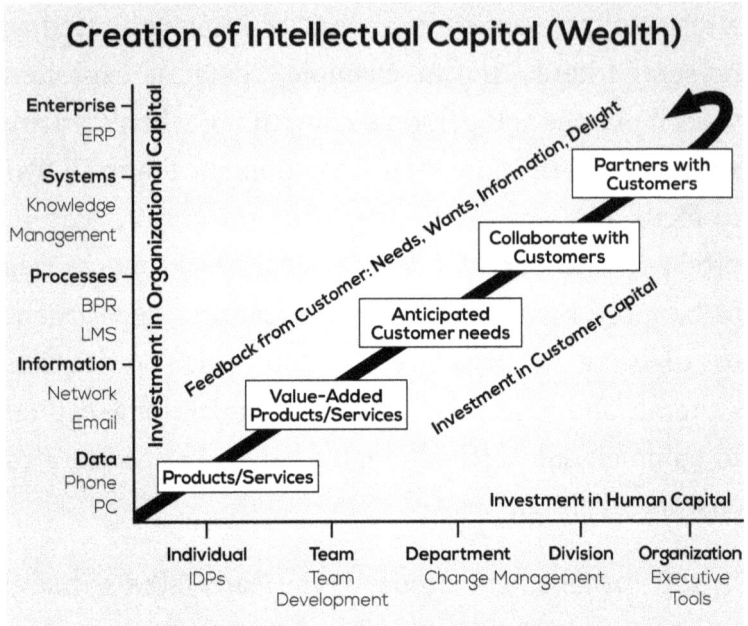

Creation of Intellectual Capital (Wealth)

©1994-2017 Baldwin H. Tom

Figure 3. Leveraging Capitals to Build Corporate Wealth

2. Investments in training and building teamwork, along with enhanced information sharing in the workplace, leads to shared ideas and *value-added products and services* to customers.

3. Investments in robust processes and procedures that cross functional silos and align with the mission of the business will reveal new opportunities to *anticipate needs of the customer*.

4. Investments in interactive systems and a change in thinking to capture the knowledge

throughout one's business will position the business as *a valuable collaborator* with its customers.

5. Investments in executives to view the business as a dynamic enterprise, plus partnering with the customer, creates the fuel that will power the business *toward industry leadership*.

Interaction of Human and Organizational Capital in Building Customer Capital

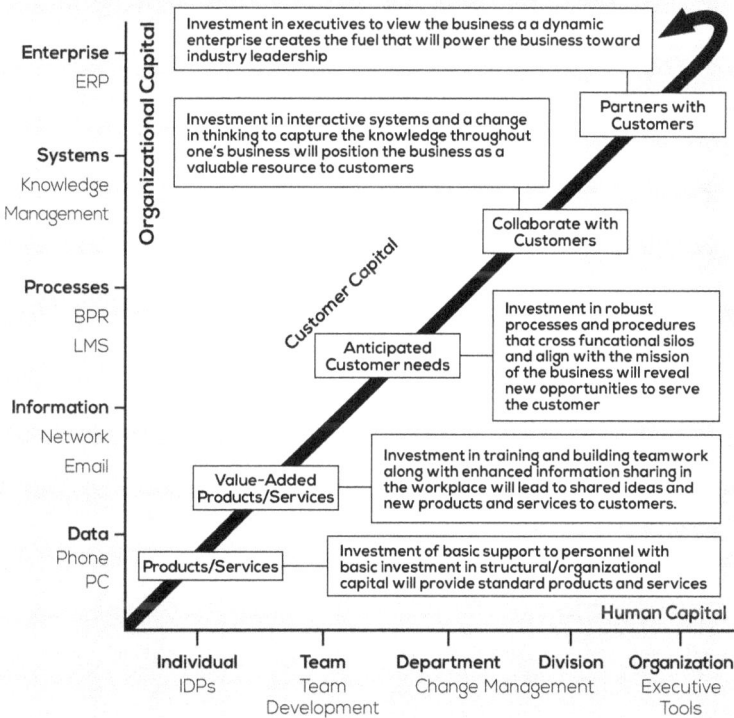

Enterprise
ERP

Organizational Capital

Investment in executives to view the business a a dynamic enterprise creates the fuel that will power the business toward industry leadership

Partners with Customers

Systems
Knowledge Management

Investment in interactive systems and a change in thinking to capture the knowledge throughout one's business will position the business as a valuable resource to customers

Collaborate with Customers

Customer Capital

Processes
BPR
LMS

Anticipated Customer needs

Investment in robust processes and procedures that cross funcational silos and align with the mission of the business will reveal new opportunities to serve the customer

Information
Network
Email

Value-Added Products/Services

Investment in training and building teamwork along with enhanced information sharing in the workplace will lead to shared ideas and new products and services to customers.

Data
Phone
PC

Products/Services

Investment of basic support to personnel with basic investment in structural/organizational capital will provide standard products and services

Human Capital

Individual
IDPs

Team
Team Development

Department
Change Management

Division

Organization
Executive Tools

©1994-2017 Baldwin H. Tom

Figure 4. Leveraging Capitals to Build Corporate Wealth

Consider for a moment that the Customer Capital diagonal is like a dial that pivots from left or right to show ROI generated by investments. And if the Customer Capital diagonal in Figure 4 is considered the maximal value you can generate with a customer (call it Vmax for maximal value and optimal ROI), we can show other dials that are less than optimal, as illustrated in Figure 5.

Here is the rationale. For every investment, there is an expected return (ROI). In this example, we are viewing the Customer as the target for investments. We can consider each successful outcome (result) for the customer as moving from one milestone to another and a modest ROI of 1 to a maximal ROI of 10 for either the Human Capital or the Organizational Capital investments. On the Organizational side, we see that the investments made in one scenario only result in a ROI of 1 (dial V_1) that doesn't change the benefits for the customer. On the Human Capital side, we see one set of investments resulting in an acceptable ROI of 4 (dial V_2) and another set of investments with an excellent ROI of 7 (dial V_3).

This depiction of the value generated by paired people and organizational investments can be shown with any set of Intellectual Capital investments, whether Relationship, Spiritual, Physical, or Financial. In the place of Customer Capital, one can seek to improve the Organizational Capital of an enterprise. Milestones might include increasing creative thinking and innovations, new inventions, more patents or trade secrets. It is not difficult to see what pairs of investments might be made to achieve these milestones. In Chapter 7 we described a number of investment groupings that lead to desired outcomes, like *creativity and innovation* for this example.

Paired Investments and ROI

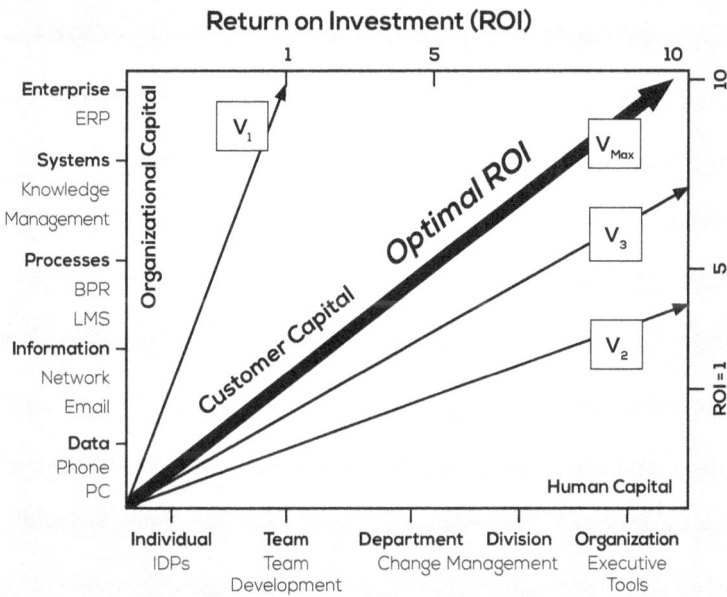

Figure 5. Charting Paired Investments and Return on Investments

The M-7 investments can be used to display the investment profile of an organization. Figure 6 plots a hypothetical diagnostic to illustrate its usefulness. The graphic shows the seven investments on a concentric graph of rings; each ring represents increasing units, from the innermost to the outermost ring. We could number these from 20 percent to 100 percent, or just a numerical set of values from 1 to 5. These rings could represent goals, targets, or milestones.

Let's say that an executive team has a retreat and develops a strategic plan to optimize their investments to improve the wealth/value of their business. They want to improve their company's ROI. For each investment area, they identify five desired outcomes (goals, targets, milestones) to be accomplished in three years. They thus mark each ring with the desired outcomes. To visualize the three-year targets, they connect the dots from each investment to the next, as shown with the broken line. They then assess their current activities and connect the dots with the solid line. This visual approach can be posted to show what has to be done to achieve the three-year plan. In this example, the patterns show the need to reduce spending on physical capital, hold the investment on financial capital, and increase investments on all other forms of capital.

Investment Diagnostic

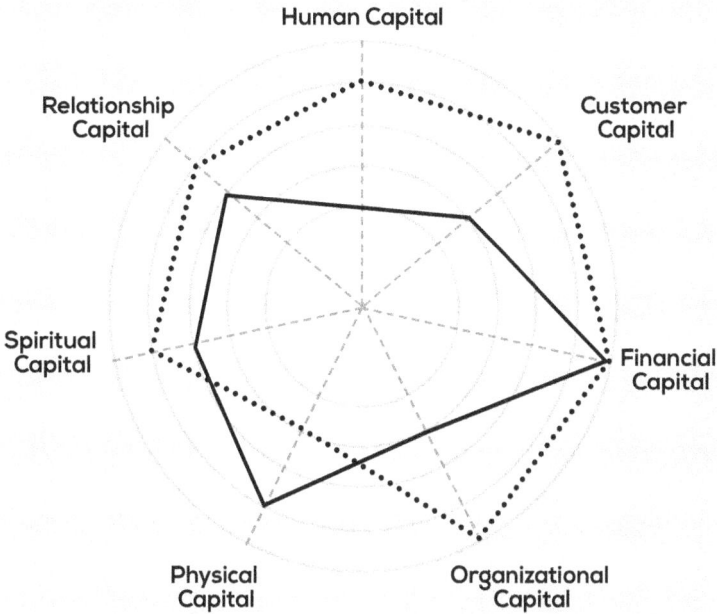

©1994-2017 Baldwin H. Tom

Figure 6. M-7 Investment Diagnostic

Financial returns and business (customer) success can be tracked in diagnostics using the seven investments.

CHAPTER 11

A NEW TOMORROW

What We Know

All actions have a people and task component and seven investments (M-7) cover most, if not all, possible investments in people and tasks. Four investments are directly people-focused, and three are task-focused. When defined as Intellectual Capital (people and people-derived outcomes), however, then five of seven (71 percent) investments are on the people side. This understanding makes it absolutely clear that people are the most important asset in a business.

Maximal ROI comes from leveraging both people and task sides. The wealth in a business comes from these investments and the success of an enterprise can thus be measured by its M-7 investments.

People-side Investments and the HR Function

When company executives fully embrace the idea that there is a real bottom line value in working with intangible assets, especially those on the people side, then the human resource executive will have equal footing with traditional corporate executives. Effectively, the HR executive will become more focused on capital generation versus people management, making hiring decisions based on talented personnel, not body count. The quality of a hire will be more important than ever before, because finding and placing star performers will be an ongoing goal. The HR executive will thereafter be expected to make stronger business cases from the human resource function. [29]

The new human resource paradigm will place the HR Director in the executive suite, helping to make strategic, company-wide economic decisions. This new paradigm has important implications, not only for the workforce, but also for the enterprise. HR professionals will need to get ready for this new economy, which will

---

[29] The concepts summarized within this section come from Thomas McGuire and Linda Brenner's enlightening book, *Talent Valuation: Accelerate Market Capitalization through Your Most Important Asset*, previously cited.

value creative, innovative, talented persons more than before, as IC produced by the talent in organizations produces its value and wealth. It becomes clear that people are the ultimate engines of business success. Thus, human capital investments (hiring, training and retention) take on system-wide economic significance.

What investments are needed to maintain a high performing workforce? In this paradigm, relationship, spiritual, and customer capitals support human capital in building wealth and sustaining high performance. Financial and physical capitals are important, but serve as foundational, sustaining functions in an enterprise.

Added Implications of M-7 Investments

The move from an industrial (machine) to a knowledge-driven (people) economy is now being finalized in business financials. The focus now shifts to the intangible side of investments and less on the tangible side. In the past, workers served machines. Today, machines serve workers. The economic relevance of people to a business's financial outcomes has changed in the past decades. Understanding necessary-versus-critical talent will be a role for the new HR executive.

Finance and HR need to reflect the new reality. Where once finance was the lynchpin connecting production with economic decision-making, a shift to human capital as the lynchpin for economic decision-making is now an imperative. It is all about connecting investments in people to value creation.

In Table 6, we provide a final look at the M-7 investments. This summary provides another perspective on the different investment groups—task, people, spiritual, financial, and customer.

TABLE 6	Summary of M-7 Investments

Investments Characteristics

Task-Side	• *Organizational Capital* includes investments into systems and processes, intellectual property, brands, and image; Facilities, hardware, machinery, and property are characterized as *physical capital. Organizational capital provides the means and accelerators that help produce knowledge. It is the memory of an enterprise.*
People-Side	• *Human capital* includes investment in knowledge, skills, and competencies. It reflects the synergies possible with diversity of culture and thought. It also includes *relationship capital* that includes the relationships built with partners, suppliers, and customers. *Human capital creates knowledge—the wealth in organizations.*
Financial Capital	• Tying the People- and Task-sides together are investments in financial and spiritual capital. *Financial capital (cash, debt, investments) provides the WD-40 lubricant to accelerate knowledge creation.*
Spiritual Capital	• Spiritual capital reflects the culture and the norms of the organization. It is the intangible input/investment from the organization that gives meaning, values, purpose, and feelings of well-being to people. *Spiritual capital provides psychic power and energy for the creation of knowledge and wealth.*
Customer Capital	• The customer is the reason for everything we do. Customer capital provides feedback and reflects the return-on-investment of all the other capitals. Investing in customer capital offers invaluable returns in fine tuning future Intellectual Capital investments.

Finally, with the emphasis on Intellectual Capital, this new valuation methodology for businesses will value intangibles more than before. We should not be surprised if we see shifts in the valuations of corporations because of shifted emphases. It will be interesting when the financial world works out the new financials that fully capture intangible value. We may be surprised when all is done.

The Engine of the Economy

Small businesses have been considered the driving force in the American economy hiring and building capacity throughout our economy. The 2015 Small Business Administration's *Profiles for the States and Territories*, notes that 57 percent of all hires are by small businesses.[30] There were 28,443,856 small businesses in 2014, and 5,707,941 of these had employees. There was a total of 56,062,893 workers employed by small businesses. American small businesses employed about half (56.1 million) of the nation's private workforce in 2012. Small businesses by necessity hire people to build their businesses, and thus, their value and wealth (human capital investment). They add infrastructure (physical investment) to support people in their work. They pair their investments. I suggest it is this direct, paired investment through which small businesses

---

[30] US Small Business Administration annual report "Small Business Profiles for the States and Territories." https://www.sba.gov/sites/default/files/advocacy/SB%20Profiles%202014-15_0.pdf.

create, per unit effort, more value and wealth for our economy than the large companies. They are truly the engines that drive the economy of the United States forward, and competitively so. Small businesses have little fluff and no time to waste human resources. They need their employees to be productive and continue to generate value. We need to support small businesses to facilitate their success.

Shifting Focus for National Health and Wealth

The first wealth is health...
RALPH WALDO EMERSON

It is obvious from the merger and acquisition discussion that the success factor was not monetary. In every case, it was about people and what they do, not the money. It is of great interest to note that in the health care industry, providers are leading the way to change the focus from monetary to nonmonetary success in treating patients. This turnaround has been driven by the federal government's mandate that health care success be measured, not by fee-for-service, but by quality of outcomes. In other words, it's not how many patients one treats, but how healthy they become. This mandate is now reinforced by reimbursement rewards and penalties. When patients have to return for treatment of the same problem within thirty days of discharge, providers are penalized.

This mandate has forced health care providers to focus on nonclinical factors that dictate healthy outcomes. These factors include both *social and physical determinants*—factors that are not part of traditional patient care. Yes, the health care industry is being forced to change for the better. The industry is investing both in people and in technology, training post-clinical professionals to support patients after clinical discharge. Its leaders are investing in technology to support patients outside of the clinic. GeoDimensional Decision Group provides a dynamic tool that supports the technology needed to integrate *social and physical determinants* of health outcomes with clinical considerations.[31] While there are different groupings of social and physical determinants by different sources, the key ones include:

- Neighborhood and built environment

- Health and health care

- Social and community context

- Education

- Economic stability

The *Healthy People 2020* website notes the following examples of social and physical determinants:[32]

---

[31] www.geoddgroup.com was cofounded by Baldwin H. Tom.

[32] USDHHS Office of Disease Prevention and Health Promotion website. "Social Determinants of Health" | Healthy People 2020. Accessed September 21, 2017.

- Availability of resources to meet daily needs (e.g., safe housing and local food markets)

- Access to educational, economic, and job opportunities

- Access to health care services

- Quality of education and job training

- Availability of community-based resources in support of community living and opportunities for recreational and leisure-time activities

- Transportation options

- Public safety

- Social support

- Social norms and attitudes (e.g., discrimination, racism, and distrust of government)

- Exposure to crime, violence, and social disorder (e.g., presence of trash and lack of cooperation in a community)

- Socioeconomic conditions (e.g., concentrated poverty and the stressful conditions that accompany it)

- Residential segregation

- Language/Literacy

https://www.healthypeople.gov/2020/topics-objectives/topic/social-determinants-of-health.

- Access to mass media and emerging technologies (e.g., cell phones, the internet, and social media)

- Culture

Physical determinants include:

- Natural environment, such as green space (e.g., trees and grass) or weather (e.g., climate change)

- Built environment, such as buildings, sidewalks, bike lanes, and roads

- Work sites, schools, and recreational settings

- Housing and community design

- Exposure to toxic substances and other physical hazards

- Physical barriers, especially for people with disabilities

- Aesthetic elements (e.g., good lighting, trees, and benches)

When the accounting world integrates Intellectual Capital into all the financial statements, the nonmonetary will be valued together with the monetary. Will the measure of our nation's financial strength be changed as well? Will we move to a Gross National Happiness (GNH) measure instead of a

Gross Domestic Product (GDP) index to measure our country's health and well-being? Such a transition would take the focus on intangible valuation to a national level.

There is a model for using the GNH. The nation of Bhutan has been using the GNH since 2008, using nonmonetary instead of monetary factors to calculate the health of their nation.[33] Bhutan's GNH is based on their four pillars to guide legislation: good governance, sustainable socioeconomic development, preservation and promotion of culture, and environmental conservation.

More germane to the United States is the United Nations' 5th World Happiness Report[34] that ranks 155 countries. Of concern is where the United States is ranked. From the Executive Summary of the report:

> *The USA is a story of reduced happiness. In 2007 the USA ranked 3rd among the OECD [U.S. Mission to the Organization for Economic Cooperation & Development] countries; in 2016 it came 19th. The reasons are declining social support and increased corruption (chapter 7) and it is these same factors that explain why the Nordic countries do so much better.*

---

[33] www.grossnationalhappiness.com

[34] www.worldhappiness.report/ed/2017

In chapter 7 of the World Happiness Report, Jeffrey D. Sachs provides an analysis around the 19th-place ranking of the United States. Sachs analyzes five factors that have caused the decline of social capital in the United States. Number five on his list is the deterioration of America's educational system, with a stagnant 36 percent of young Americans completing a bachelor's degree or higher. This also reflects fewer students going on to college. Sachs concludes, "America has lost the edge in educating its citizens for the 21st century; that fact alone ensures a social crisis that will continue to threaten well-being until the commitment to quality education for all is once again a central tenet of American society."

Final question: Would the emphasis on valuing intangibles on spreadsheets that casts a fresh focus on the importance of people as drivers of wealth in organizations change the urgency for more robust educational experiences for our children and adults?

An emphasis on the importance of people side investments and the elevated role of the human resource function dictates future changes in how we measure enterprise and even national wealth.

APPENDIX A:

ABOUT THE AUTHOR

While taking an unplanned career path, Baldwin H. Tom has excelled in three careers, receiving recognition and awards in each. His parents wanted him to become a doctor. He started as a medical school research scientist/professor (Stanford, Northwestern, and University of Texas Houston) and left with some acclaim. In this medical career, he had sixty publications, received a patent for a cancer diagnostic, was awarded a National Cancer Institute Research Career Development Award, was a visiting scholar at the University of Nottingham in the United Kingdom, and cofounded a NASA-funded space bioprocessing research institute.

Baldwin did not have the passion to stay in medical research, so when given a chance, he followed up with a ten-year stint as a leadership director and trainer, creating three leadership programs, with one winning a national award. He served a term as the executive director of the American Leadership Forum.

Baldwin is a Certified Management Consultant and served as the National Board Chair of the Institute of

Management Consultants USA (IMC) and a United Nations Trustee for the International Council of Management Consulting Institutes. He was recognized as a Fellow of the IMC. He earned his BA degree in biochemistry from the University of California, a PhD in biochemistry/immunology from the University of Arizona and an MBA in organizational development from Houston Baptist University.

In his career as an entrepreneur, he started four businesses. The Baldwin Group (TBG), a consulting firm he cofounded with his wife, has outlasted all of them for more than twenty-eight years. A prolific blogger on diverse topics, he published the first paper characterizing the problems of not only exceeding one's competency (Peter Principle) but also exceeding one's compatibility (Doss Principle) in a position/job. His most recent venture was cofounding a new company, GeoDimensional Decision Group (GeoDD).

Baldwin sang tenor with the Houston Masterworks Chorus and the National Men's Chorus in Washington, DC. At age seventy, he started competing as a paddler on a dragon boat team. At seventy-four, he tried out for the over-60 US National Dragon Boat Team of twenty-four paddlers. He was 27th and missed the cut. He hasn't given up paddling, but has since taken up golf and wants to be competitive. By the way, he intends to break 100 in golf and live to 100.

Baldwin has two adult children and lives with his wife in the San Francisco Bay Area.

APPENDIX B
WORKS REFERENCED

Adamopoulos, Helen. "Report: 3 Key Healthcare Merger and Acquisition Trends." *Becker's Hospital Review*, 21 Nov. 2013, www.beckershospitalreview. com/hospital-transactions-and-valuation/report-3-key-healthcare-merger-and-acquisition-trends.html.

Arango, Tim. "How the AOL-Time Warner Merger Went So Wrong." *The New York Times*, The New York Times, 10 Jan. 2010, www.nytimes.com/2010/01/11/business/media/11merger.html.

"Articles and Advice for College Students & Graduates." *Experience*, www.experience.com/. Accessed 21 Sept. 2017.

Biery, Mary Ellen Research Specialist. "7 Aspects of Your CPA Firm Culture That Can Make or Break a Merger." *Sageworks*, 14 July 2014, www.sageworks. com/blog/post/2016/07/14/7-aspects-of-your-cpa-firm-culture-that-can-make-or-break-a-merger.aspx.

"Big 4 Accounting Firms—Who They Are, Facts and Information." *Accountingverse.com*, www.accounting

verse.com/articles/big-4-accounting-firms.html. Accessed 21 Sept. 2017.

"Biotech and Big Pharma: Keys to a Successful M&A." *FTI Journal*, Jan. 2016, www.ftijournal.com/article/biotech-and-big-pharma-keys-to-a-successful-m-and-a. Accessed 21 Sept. 2017.

Christensen, Clayton M., Richard Alton, Curtis Rising, and Andrew Waldeck. "The Big Idea: The New M&A Playbook." *Harvard Business Review*, March 2011

Dyrda, Laura. "8 Trends in Healthcare Mergers & Acquisitions for 2017." *Becker's ASC Review*, 10 Jan. 2017, www.beckersasc.com/asc-transactions-and-valuation-issues/8-trends-in-healthcare-mergers-acquisitions-for-2017.html.

Edvinsson, Leif and Michael S. Malone. *Intellectual Capital: Realizing Your Company's True Value by Finding its Hidden Brainpower*. Harper Business Press, New York, 1997.

Evans, Peter, et al. "Measuring Organizational Capital." *The Center for Global Enterprise*, 24 Feb. 2016, thecge.net/category/research/measuring-organizational-capital/.

Forbes Leadership Forum. "Why Half of All M&A Deals Fail, and What You Can Do About It." Forbes,

9 Oct. 2014, www.forbes.com/sites/forbesleadership-
forum/2012/03/19/why-half-of-all-ma-deals-fail-and-
what-you-can-do-about-it/.

Galbraith, John Kenneth. *The New Industrial State.*
Houghton Mifflin, Boston, 1967.

Gallup, Inc. "Three Prescriptions for Successful
Healthcare Mergers." *Gallup.com*, 19 Nov. 2014,
www.gallup.com/businessjournal/179486/three-
prescriptions-successful-healthcare-mergers.aspx.

"Gross National Happiness." Centre for Buhtan
Studies and GNH, www.grossnationalhappiness.com.
Accessed 21 Sept. 2017

International Accounting System 38.8 definition of
intangible asset. International Financial Reporting
Standards (IFRS). https://www.iasplus.com/en/
standards/ias/ias38

Landi, Heather. "Looking at Hospital M&A Activity
in the Value-Based Care World." *Healthcare Informatics
Magazine*, 11 Nov. 2016, www.healthcare-informatics.
com/article/payment/looking-hospital-ma-activity-
value-based-care-world.

Magrassi, Paolo. "A Taxonomy of Intellectual Capital." 2002. Gartner.com.

McGuire, Thomas, and Linda Brenner. *Talent Valuation: Accelerate Market Capitalization through Your Most Important Asset*. Pearson Education LTD, 2015.

"Salesforce Integration Generates M&A Success in Healthcare." Bain & Company, June 2017, www.bain.com/about/client-results/salesforce-integration-generates-m-and-a-success-in-healthcare.aspx. Accessed 21 Sept. 2017.

Schmidt, Peter J. "Key Tips for a Successful Hospital Merger or Acquisition." *Healthcare Finance News*, 2 July 2015, www.healthcarefinancenews.com/blog/key-tips-successful-hospital-merger-or-acquisition.

Schramski, Tom. "7 Issues Healthcare CEOs Should Consider Before Engaging in M&A." *Axial*, 10 May 2016, www.axial.net/forum/7-issues-healthcarehealthcare-ceos-consider-engaging-ma/.

Sinkin, Joel, and Terrence Putney. "The Culture Test." *Journal of Accountancy*, 1 May 2014, www.journalofaccountancy.com/issues/2014/may/20139298.html.

Tom, Baldwin H. and Ian C. Jacobsen. "Peter Principle Meets Doss Principle: Secrets for Engaging Consultants to Management." National Contract Management Association's *Journal of Contract Management*, Feb. 2006, 42-47.

Tsokanos, Jim. "9 Ways to Help Make Health Care Provider M&As Successful." *Jim Tsokanos.net,* 29 Nov. 2016, jimtsokanos.net/9-ways-help-make-health-care-provider-mas-successful/.

USDHHS Office of Disease Prevention and Health Promotion website. "Social Determinants of Health." *Healthy People 2020,* www.healthypeople.gov/2020/topics-objectives/topic/social-determinants-of-health. Accessed 21 Sept. 2017.

US Small Business Administration annual report "Small Business Profiles for the States and Territories." https://www.sba.gov/sites/default/files/advocacy/SB%20Profiles%202014-15_0.pdf.

Valentine, Steven, and Daniel Juberg. "Top 10 Pivotal Factors for Successful Mergers and Acquisitions." GE Healthcare Camden Group, Oct. 2015, www.thecamdengroup.com/thought-leadership/top-ten/top-10-pivotal-factors-for-successful-mergers-and-acquisitions/.

"What Is Intellectual Capital? Definition and Meaning." BusinessDictionary.com, www.businessdictionary.com/definition/intellectual-capital.html.

"What is Relationship Capital?" Related Vision. Accessed 22 Oct. 2017. http://www.relatedvision.com/Relationship-Capital/relationship-capital.html

Wootton, Charles W, and Carel M Wolk. "The Development of 'The Big Eight' Accounting Firms in the United States, 1900 to 1990." *Accounting Historians Journal,* www.accountingin.com/accounting-historians-journal/volume-19-number-1/the-development-of-the-big-eight-accounting-firms-in-the-united-states-1900-to-1990/. Accessed 21 Sept. 2017.

"World Happiness Report 2017." *World Happiness Report,* www.worldhappiness.report/ed/2017. Accessed 21 Sept. 2017.

Yanci, Jim, et al. "What Hospital Executives Should Be Considering in Hospital Mergers and Acquisitions." *Dixon Hughes Goodman,* 2013, www2.dhgllp.com/res_pubs/Hospital-Mergers-and-Acquisitions.pdf. Accessed 21 Sept. 2017.

ACKNOWLEDGMENTS

God is my copilot. Everyone is on a journey. Along the way we make turns for our career, family, and life's purpose. Oftentimes we have no idea why we are led to head in a specific direction when it doesn't make sense, or, worse, seems a dead end. Until we gain perspective by living life and reflecting, we are hard pressed to connect the dots of our lives. Today I can see clearly, or at least I have what I consider valid reasons, why I took certain turns in work and life. Amazingly, all the zigs and zags in my life now make sense; I am connecting the dots.

While I come from a Christian family traced back to my grandfather who emigrated from China in the late 1890s, I considered myself a Christian only on forms for most of my life, meaning that I attended church twice a year, at Easter and Christmas. It was only in the past twenty years that I became serious in attending church each Sunday.

There is no longer doubt in my mind that my life path has been guided by supernatural forces. I have witnessed many miracles in my life and do not ignore a God who has led me through bad times and good times. All these life opportunities have made me who I am. So I thank God for leading me through the wilderness of life to this point.

Wife and family. After more than fifty years of marriage, I can safely say that my wife, Madeline, and I are compatible (most of the time). If you checked our personality styles with Myers-Briggs or DiSC tools, you will find we are total opposites. While opposites attract, I did not appreciate what that meant. Opposites have the most difficult time to build a relationship because each sees the opposite side of almost all situations. For example, I am a driver type, wanting to get things done *now*. Madeline is a sensing type person, wanting to take time to look over the situation before moving on. Simply, I'm more pushy; she is not. She cares more about people, I care more about things. This means that I am very task-oriented, regardless of what people think, while she cares a lot about what people think.

Guess what? When opposites understand that each has complementary strengths and weaknesses, and if they work together, they become a powerful force! Just like a positive and negative magnetic force placed together, this makes a very strong bond. Madeline has been wife, partner, and opposite force for me to fine-tune who I have become. Yes, we're still a work in progress, but I love her forever.

Our children, Darren and Alyson, continue to check on us to make sure we are well and thriving. Madeline and I are very proud of them. Each is special and successful. We wanted them to become independent, self-sufficient, and contributing members of society. They are doing just that. We look forward to the day when they, too, will be able to connect the dots of their journeys. Love you both!

While my parents were killed in a terrorist attack more than fifty years ago in service to the CIA, we know they are pleased with what their son has accomplished. I thank them for setting the example of hard work, never quitting, loving the family, and leaving me in God's hands.

Church and friends. Life is a challenging journey. Life without other people is even more so. Learning from others and having sounding boards makes living less challenging and more enjoyable. I know that I am a better person in all ways because of my interactions with others. People challenge my ideas, validate them, and enhance them. The end results are always better. Many of those people are from my spiritual, intangible side. These folks can communicate with me in more supernatural, spiritual ways and I understand their message. This group has helped me to weather life's storms that invariably rise up. Dr. Mark Batterson, lead pastor at National Community Church, provided many sermons that reached me deeply and was an inspiration through his many published works. Because of his messages, I have grown deeper in my faith journey and am better able to deal with the challenges of life.

Other people who have been blessings to me are from the business, tangible side. Joe Synan, when president of the American Leadership Forum reached out to me (at a time when I was not-so-politely asked to find a new career from the university where I worked at the time) and asked me to apply for the executive director's position. I had no experience leading a nonprofit, but was selected anyway to lead the chapter in Houston. I am grateful for them, as each has contributed to the trajectory of my life's journey.

One key person that helped us move from a boutique consulting practice into a successful, full-fledged, and thriving business was Ron Perlman. In our first-ever meeting with Ron, he "adopted" us after we moved from Houston to Washington, DC. Our focus in Houston was consulting in the corporate world, and Ron guided us into a very different federal contracting world. For twelve years he successfully shepherded us, instructing us about the nuances around federal contracts. Our current journey would have been much more difficult without him. We are very grateful for his unswerving support during those years.

I also want to thank the following individuals for their presence and help on my journey from academician to leadership/management consultant, and from scientist to small business owner: famed management consultant and author Alan Weiss, who served with me on the board of directors of the Institute of Management Consultants USA; international consultant Dr. Zlática Kraljevic, a colleague and author of the outstanding book *Borderless Leadership,* about international business; former Houston Mayor Dr. Lee P. Brown, the author of *Community Policing,* a friend for forty years who served as a respected police chief in Atlanta, New York City and Houston and as President Bill Clinton's Drug Czar; founder of the American Leadership Forum (ALF) Joe Jaworski, son of Watergate prosecutor Leon Jaworski, and the man I was proud to serve as the first executive director of the Houston Gulf Coast Chapter of the ALF; Vice President Linda O'Black of the United Way of the Texas Gulf Coast, who supported me for ten years in leading Project Blueprint, an award-winning leadership program; and pastor and Governor Mike Huckabee, who inspired me with his dedication to his church and country in Niceville, Florida, where I visited. Finally, thank you, Michael Pai, for capturing the theme of each chapter with cartoon figures. Michael trained with Disney animators.